★ 2016 AND BEYOND ★

2016 and Beyond: How Republicans Can Elect a President in the New America
Whit Ayres
ISBN 978-1-927967-39-3

Published by Resurgent Republic
www.ResurgentRepublic.com

Graphics: Cheryl Martin Glenn
Editing: Lesley Dahl
Cover Design: Jayme Brewer

Produced by IndieBookLauncher.com
www.IndieBookLauncher.com

Copy Editing: Nassau Hedron
Book Design and Typesetting: Saul Bottcher

The body text of this book is set in Caslon by Adobe. Chapter Headings are set in Myriad by Adobe and Museo Sans by exljbris. Section headings are set in Liberation Sans by Red Hat.

Also Available
EPUB edition ISBN 978-1-927967-40-9
Kindle edition ISBN 978-1-927967-41-6

To Angela

*Without her constant encouragement and support, this
book would never have come to fruition*

2016 AND BEYOND
HOW REPUBLICANS CAN ELECT
A PRESIDENT IN THE NEW AMERICA

WHIT AYRES

CONTENTS

ACKNOWLEDGMENTS

I owe a debt of gratitude to numerous people who have helped develop and interpret the public opinion research on which this book is based, but none more so than my work family at North Star Opinion Research.

Cheryl Martin Glenn devoted endless hours to creating the graphs, formatting the book, and using her eagle eye to spot errors and passages needing clarification. Her dedication to this project is unsurpassed, and I cannot imagine writing this book or running our business without her.

Jon McHenry is one of our profession's leading pollsters and methodologists. In addition to being a technological wizard, he has a remarkable gift for creating visual displays that make complicated quantitative data readily accessible and understandable.

Dan Judy has rapidly become one of our profession's most talented focus group moderators and analysts of polling data. He has a real knack for getting quickly to the heart of a problem, and his judgment and strategic advice are consistently wise and insightful.

In addition to their thorough professionalism, the camaraderie and good humor of my North Star colleagues makes our office a wonderful place to work and explore the fascinating game of American politics.

Lesley Dahl is a most talented copy editor who helped to clarify the arguments and make my points more persuasive. Even more important, she became an ambassador for this project, believing in its purpose and offering valuable advice.

Saul Bottcher provided excellent guidance through the intricacies of publishing and made a number of helpful suggestions. Nas Hedron carefully proofed the final draft and provided sound stylistic suggestions.

Jayme Brewer created the cover design to symbolize the book's message, and patiently tolerated numerous tweaks and suggestions.

As co-founder of Resurgent Republic, Ed Gillespie provided the inspiration and raised the money to get the organization off the ground, which allowed us to develop much of the data presented here. During his 2014 run for the U.S. Senate from Virginia, he demonstrated that a great Republican candidate can unify our party and extend its appeal to all demographic groups in a diverse state.

Resurgent Republic would never have existed without the generosity of our donors, who believed in the mission of creating fresh, new, center-right messaging for a 21st century audience.

Special thanks to Governor Haley Barbour who ably served as Resurgent Republic's interim President during Ed's absence, Luke Frans, our first executive director, and Leslie Sanchez, a specialist on immigration policy and fellow Resurgent Republic Board member. In addition, I appreciate the contributions of my Republican pollster colleagues and competitors whose many hours of focus groups for Resurgent Republic contributed to the strategic advice offered in this book: Glen Bolger, Linda DiVall, Ed Goeas, Jan van Lohuizen, and John McLaughlin.

Notwithstanding the contributions of these and many other people, the interpretations of the data and the strategic advice offered are, for better or worse, mine and mine alone.

★ INTRODUCTION ★

PUBLIC OPINION *and a* NEW REPUBLICAN MESSAGE

Few midterm elections have yielded as many impressive Republican victories as 2010 and 2014. In 2010 the party picked up 63 seats in the House of Representatives, the largest number of seats gained in a midterm election since 1938. Republicans added 6 more seats in the U.S. Senate, 6 additional governorships, and 680 seats in state legislatures across the country.

2014 was, if possible, even more impressive. Republicans took control of the Senate by winning 9 new seats, in the process defeating 5 Democratic incumbents, the largest number since 1980. Republicans expanded their House majority by 14 seats, and achieved the greatest Republican majority since 1928.[1] They reelected all but 2 of their Republican governors, often by substantial margins, and added Republican governors in the deep blue states of Illinois, Massachusetts, and Maryland. Republican gains extended far down the ballot, controlling 69 of the 99 state legislative chambers, 31 lieutenant governorships, and 28 secretaries of state.[2] Republicans control both chambers of the state legislature in 30 states, and control both the legislature and governor's office in 23 states.[3]

If only Republicans had been equally successful in presidential elections. Despite all their success in midterms, Republicans have been unsuccessful at winning presidential elections for a decade, losing twice to resolutely liberal Barack Obama by landslide margins in the Electoral College.

---

1. After the election, Republican congressman Michael Grimm resigned leaving one vacancy to be filled by a special election.

2. *http://www.rslc.gop/take_a_look_at_republican_gains_since_2010*

3. *http://cookpolitical.com/story/8145*

Republicans have lost the popular vote in five of the last six presidential elections.

Why can't Republicans, who have been so successful in midterm elections, be equally successful in presidential elections?

Numerous commentators weighed in on that question after the last loss to Obama in 2012. The problem was variously deemed to be poor communications or outdated technology or bad candidates or bad consultants or poor strategy or rigid ideology or too many primaries or too many debates or a hostile media or too much bickering among the faithful.

Under the leadership of Republican National Committee Chairman Reince Priebus, in 2013 the RNC's Growth and Opportunity Project weighed in with a tough report providing recommendations in many of these areas. But the report shied away from making many policy recommendations, because policy is presumably the province of candidates, not the party structure. While many of the recommendations of that project will help Republican fortunes in presidential elections in the future, no analysis is complete without tackling policy positions and the broader Republican message.

That is especially critical given that polling clearly indicates that the Republican victories in 2010 and 2014 were largely a repudiation of the Democratic message and not an endorsement of a Republican alternative. Only 16 percent of Americans said the 2014 Republican victory was a "mandate for Republicans," while 74 percent thought it was a "rejection of Democrats."[4] By a margin of 54 to 42 percent, 2014 midterm voters had an unfavorable view of the Republican Party, comparable to the 55 to 43 percent unfavorable view they held of the Democratic Party.[5]

---

4. CNN/ORC survey November 21-23, 2014, as quoted in The Hill, December 8, 2014, p. 8

5. *http://www.foxnews.com/politics/elections/2014/exit-polls*

Our approach here looks to public opinion as a guide to craft a new Republican message that will resonate more effectively with the nation's voters in the 21st century presidential elections. What do voters think about the Republicans' message and issue positions? Do Americans still lean center-right in their political views? What do voters want out of government? Have their desires changed significantly since Barack Obama was elected president? What do Republican presidential candidates need to do to appeal to a broader swath of the national electorate?

Our purpose here is not to "follow the polls" as critics so derisively put it. No poll will ever substitute for the wisdom and judgment of foresighted leaders. No focus group will ever definitively point the way forward for a complex foreign policy dilemma. Public opinion can be remarkably informed, stable, and sophisticated on some issues, yet disturbingly uninformed, unstable, and simplistic on others.

Nevertheless, in a democratic political system, public opinion always deserves a respectful hearing. As Abraham Lincoln said, "Our government rests in public opinion. Whoever can change public opinion can change the government, practically just so much." He added, "In this and like communities, public sentiment is everything. With public sentiment, nothing can fail; without it, nothing can succeed."[6]

We will examine the presidential travails of today's Republican Party through the perspective of public opinion. It seems the least we should do in a government "of the people, by the people, and for the people."

That task inevitably involves looking at public opinion data. We will try to do so in a way that tells a story and paints a picture, rather than by presenting mountains of data or pages of tables. Whenever possible we will use graphs and pictures rather than tables. We will rely on examples of typical public opinion responses, often those developed by our own

---

6.   http://quod.lib.umich.edu/j/jala/2629860.0015.204/--public-sentiment-is-everything-lincolns-view-of-political?rgn=main;view=fulltext

polling firm, rather than presenting an exhaustive review of every recently asked question on a topic. Our hope is to be true to the recent findings of public opinion research and make them readily comprehensible for a lay audience.

We do not pretend to find one "correct" answer, because there is no single answer on each of the issues facing the country. There is no one perfect combination of economic, social, and foreign policy stands that will create a surefire winning formula in a presidential election. We do hope to offer a sense of the directions that are promising for the future, and identify those that are dead ends in a 21st century electorate.

The redefinition of the Republican message will not be complete until the party selects its 2016 nominee for president. That nominee, and the mix of issue positions he or she holds, will define the new Republican message. And if that nominee wins the presidency, the positions he or she holds will define the new Republican Party.

We hope to light a candle rather than just curse the darkness. A bit of cursing will be necessary to understand the depth of the hole Republicans have dug for themselves in presidential elections. Ultimately, our goal is to light the way forward to a brighter day and a brighter future for Republicans, for the presidency, and for the country.

THE CHALLENGE

The Republican Party has lost five of the last six presidential elections in the popular vote, and four of the last six in the Electoral College. Demographic groups that form the core of Republican support—older whites, blue-collar whites, married people, and rural residents—are declining as a proportion of the electorate. Demographic groups where the party is weak—minorities, young people, single women—are growing.

The uncomfortable reality is that the Republican Party has a worn out business model for a 21st-century presidential electorate. What once sold so effectively is no longer persuasive to the majority of voters who elect a president. And without controlling the presidency, Republicans will never be able to advance their national agenda and turn the country in a different direction.

That argument seems incongruous in light of the stunning Republican successes up and down the ballot in the 2014 midterms. The 2014 results make it seem as though the Republican business model is alive and well, dominating government in large and important regions of the country. But consider the following:

- Republican congressional candidates won 60 percent of white voters[7] in both 2010 and 2014, a level sufficient to win landslide victories in both years.

---

7. Throughout this book, "white" refers to non-Hispanic whites, those who do not consider themselves to be of Hispanic or Latino origin.

- Republican presidential nominee Mitt Romney won 59 percent of white voters in 2012, and still lost the election by five million votes.[8]

Clearly presidential electorates are different from midterm electorates in fundamental ways, ways that work to the disadvantage of Republican presidential candidates.

The danger is that Republican successes in 2010 and 2014 will disguise the long-term problems facing the Republican Party, and postpone the changes that need to occur for Republicans to elect a president. In the long run, the Republican Party is in trouble in presidential elections unless something changes.

Weak Performance Among Racial Minorities

In 2012 Mitt Romney won by a landslide among white voters, 59 to 39 percent. Romney received the highest percentage of the white vote of any Republican candidate challenging an incumbent president in the history of exit polling, surpassing even Ronald Reagan's percentage among whites in his 1980 victory over Jimmy Carter. Romney won every significant white subgroup, often by overwhelming margins—men and women, young and old, Protestants and Catholics.

---

8. I am indebted to Ron Brownstein, the excellent National Journal reporter, who first posed this dilemma so starkly.

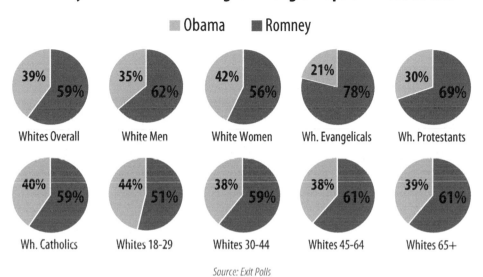

Romney vs. Obama Percentages Among Groups of White Voters

Obama   Romney

Whites Overall — 39% / 59%

White Men — 35% / 62%

White Women — 42% / 56%

Wh. Evangelicals — 21% / 78%

Wh. Protestants — 30% / 69%

Wh. Catholics — 40% / 59%

Whites 18-29 — 44% / 51%

Whites 30-44 — 38% / 59%

Whites 45-64 — 38% / 61%

Whites 65+ — 39% / 61%

Source: Exit Polls

Figure 1-1

Even so, Romney's dominance among whites was insufficient to craft a national majority in the America of 2012 because Barack Obama won breathtaking majorities among every other racial group. Obama won near-unanimous support among African-Americans, along with almost three-to-one support among Hispanics and Asians, and a 20-point margin among voters of other racial categories. Consequently, the first African-American president won reelection with the support of only four out of ten white voters.

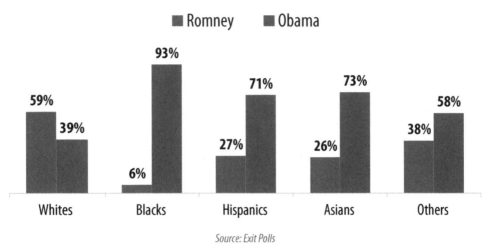

Romney vs. Obama Percentages Among Racial Groups

■ Romney   ■ Obama

Source: Exit Polls

Figure 1-2

The challenge facing Republicans is obvious. Trying to win a presidential election by gaining a larger and larger share of the vote from a smaller and smaller share of the electorate is a losing political proposition.

Weak Performance Among Younger and Northern Whites

The Republican challenge goes beyond demographics and weak support among racial minorities. Romney seriously underperformed among young people and northern whites, especially those in the electoral-vote-rich states of the upper Midwest.

While Romney did win white voters under age 30, he did so by only 7 percentage points, 51 to 44 percent, compared to margins of 21 percentage points or more among whites age 30 and older. In the 2014 midterm election, Republican candidates for the House of Representatives performed somewhat better among whites under age 30, winning them by 11 points, 54 to 43 percent. But that is still less than the 18 points or more by which Republicans won whites age 30 and older in 2014. Younger white voters are still up for grabs politically, but relatively weak support for Republicans among younger whites is disturbing in the long term.

Romney's landslide among white voters nationally is distorted by his huge margins among whites in deep red states. As the chart below demonstrates, in the battleground states that decided the 2012 election, Romney's performance among whites lagged his national numbers.

Romney Percentages Among White Voters in States With Exit Polls

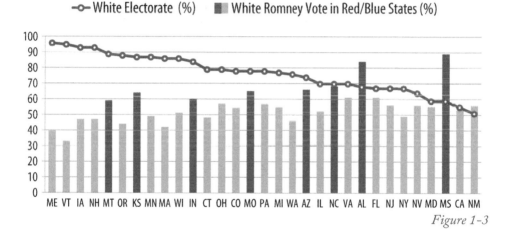

Figure 1-3

Not all states are represented in this chart, just those with state-level exit polls in 2012. But the pattern is clear: Romney received overwhelming margins of the white vote in southern states like Mississippi, Alabama, and North Carolina; Midwestern states like Missouri, Indiana, and Kansas; and western states like Arizona and Montana. But Romney won fewer than half the white votes in some of the "whitest" states in the country, such as Maine, Vermont, Iowa, New Hampshire, and Oregon, and fewer than he needed to carry Wisconsin, Michigan, Minnesota, Ohio, and Pennsylvania.

For Republicans to become competitive again in presidential elections, Republican candidates must perform better among whites, especially in the overwhelmingly white states of the upper Midwest, and much better among minorities.

It is always tempting for partisans to blame the presidential candidate and his campaign for a significant loss. Mitt Romney and his team certainly deserve their share of the blame. Tone-deaf comments by the nominee, technological deficiencies, and curious strategic decision-making all contributed to losing a campaign that at one point seemed winnable.

Placing all the blame on the candidate and his campaign is too easy, however, and avoids facing the more fundamental problems confronting the Republican Party. Romney and his campaign explain losing the popular vote in one out of six presidential elections, but not five out of six. Republicans' difficulties electing a president go to the essence of the Republican message and its appeal to the electorate of the 21st century.

The Halcyon Days of Yore

It was not always this way. Not so long ago, Republicans held a virtual lock on the presidency. Comparing two 20-year periods starkly shows the deterioration in Republican fortunes in presidential elections.

Percent of the Popular Vote for President: 1968-2012

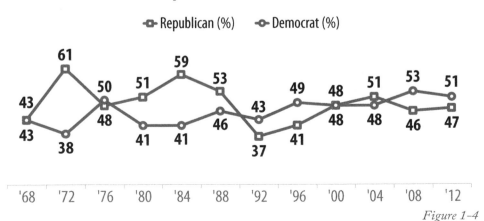

Figure 1-4

In the six presidential elections from 1968 to 1988, Republicans won the popular vote by an average of 8.2 million votes and 9.58 percentage points, in the process winning five of the six presidential elections during the period. The only blemish on the record occurred during the Watergate hangover when Gerald Ford lost to Jimmy Carter in 1976. Yet even that one loss was close—Ford lost by only 2 percentage points, 48 to 50 percent. Ford came closer to defeating Jimmy Carter in 1976 than Mitt Romney came to unseating Barack Obama in 2012.

In the six presidential elections from 1992 to 2012, however, the story is dramatically different. Republicans lost the popular vote over that period by an average of 4.3 million votes, a net swing from the first period of 12.5 million votes. The average percentage loss for Republicans was 3.87 percentage points, or a net swing of 13.45 percentage points downward compared to the first period.

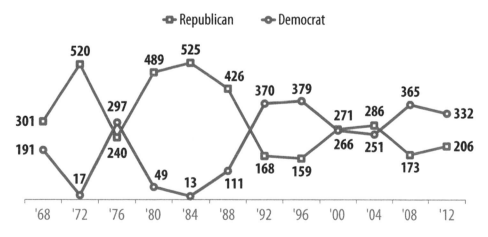

Electoral Votes for President: 1968–2012

Note: George Wallace received 46 electoral votes in 1968.

Figure 1-5

The picture painted by the Electoral College is bleaker and, from a Republican perspective, even more frightening. Other than the 1976 loss, Republicans completely dominated the Electoral College between 1968 and 1988, winning an average of 417 electoral votes over the period, 147 more than the 270 necessary to win the presidency. (The average would have been higher still had George Wallace not won 46 electoral votes in 1968, votes that likely would have gone to Richard Nixon.) Republican dominance was so complete during the period that their *margin of victory* surpassed 300 electoral votes in four of the six elections.

From 1992 to 2012, Republican dominance of the Electoral College evaporated. In the six most recent elections, Republican presidential candidates won an average of only 211 electoral votes, 59 shy of those necessary to elect a president. Not once did a Republican candidate for president surpass 300 electoral votes, a bar crossed five times in the prior period. Indeed, the 240 electoral votes won by Ford in his losing 1976 effort surpassed the Republican total in four of the six most recent presidential campaigns.

Republican Electoral Votes Advantage or Disadvantage: 1968-2012

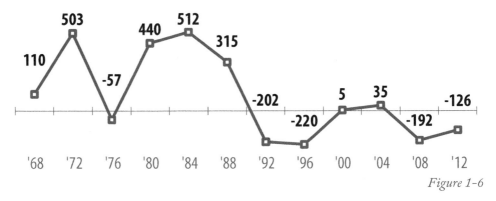

Figure 1-6

The trend line in the Republican advantage or disadvantage in the Electoral College is ominous. Unless something is done to change the trend, Republican candidates will no longer even be competitive in presidential elections.

Problem? What Problem?

From the perspective of Republicans in the deepest red states, Republicans do not have major problems. Or if they do, it is because Republican presidential nominees in recent years have been insufficiently conservative. Red-state Republicans fear that if the Republican Party changes to appeal more to racial minorities and young people, it will undermine their strength in the states they now dominate.

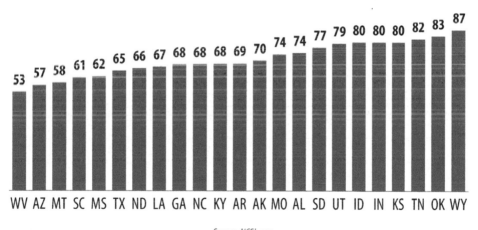

Percentage of Republican-Held Seats in State Senates After the 2014 Midterm Election in States Romney Won in 2012

Source: NCSL.org

Figure 1-7

And dominate is the right word. Consider the proportion of Republicans in the state senate chambers in states won by Romney in 2012 after the 2014 election. Republicans control 20 of the 23 state senates with 60 percent or more of the seats, and 11 of the 23 with 70 percent or more[9] (Nebraska's unicameral legislature is excluded from the chart).

Dominance is not confined to the Deep South. In Tennessee, a border state whose voters have sent pragmatic Republican conservatives like

---

9. National Conference of State Legislatures

Lamar Alexander and Bob Corker to the U.S. Senate, and Bill Haslam to the governor's mansion, Republicans now control the state senate by 27 seats to 6, and the state house by 73 seats to 26.[10] Republicans control the governor's office, all statewide elected officials, both U.S. Senate seats, and 7 of 9 congressional seats.

When you have control and are increasing your margin of control, why make any changes? As an elected official, why open the door to a Republican primary challenge from the right?

Because the total number of electoral college votes represented by the 23 states in the chart above constitutes only 201 votes, far shy of the 270 needed to win the presidency. If Republicans don't become more competitive in the Electoral College, Democrats will control the presidency and the ability to chart the country's direction as far as the eye can see.

We've Been Here Before

A political party appearing to be on the ropes as a national force is nothing new. The prospect facing Republicans today bears striking similarities to that facing the Democratic Party in 1989. Democrats at the time controlled both houses of Congress, but they were just coming off another Republican shellacking in a presidential contest, their fifth overwhelming electoral college loss in six elections.

The Democrat's left wing appeared to have a stranglehold on the message and direction of the party, producing liberal nominees like Walter Mondale in 1984 and Michael Dukakis in 1988, both of whom were out of step with the thinking of most Americans. Many Democrats resisted any fundamental reexamination of their message and appeal to a broader electorate. Even in the face of those two whopping losses, Democrats were still reluctant to reexamine their message.

---

10. Ibid

Then along came two political scientists: William Galston of the University of Maryland and Elaine Ciulla Kamarck of the Progressive Policy Institute. Galston and Kamarck produced a paper that was, at the time, extraordinarily controversial. The paper, with its combative title, "The Politics of Evasion: Democrats and the Presidency," posed an aggressive challenge to the then establishment thinking in the Democratic Party.[11]

Some passages are eerily similar to the Republican predicament today:

> *Democrats have ignored their fundamental problems. Instead of facing reality they have embraced the politics of evasion. They have focused on fundraising and technology, media and momentum, personality and tactics. Worse, they have manufactured excuses for their presidential disasters—excuses built on faulty data and false assumptions, excuses designed to avoid tough questions. In place of reality they have offered wishful thinking; in place of analysis, myth.*

> *This systematic denial of reality—the politics of evasion—continues unabated today, years after the collapse of the liberal majority and the New Deal alignment. Its central purpose is the avoidance of meaningful change. It reflects the convictions of groups who believed that it is somehow immoral for a political party to pay attention to public opinion. It reflects the interests of those who would rather be the majority in a minority party than risk being the minority in a majority party.*

Galston and Kamarck pointed to reflexive liberalism at the core of the Democrats' dilemma:

> *The oldest of these myths is that Democrats have lost presidential elections because they have strayed from traditional liberal orthodoxy. The perpetrators of this myth greet any deviation from liberal dogma,*

---

11. *http://www.progressivepolicy.org/wp-content/uploads/2013/03/Politics_of_ Evasion.pdf*

any attempt at innovation with the refrain "We don't need two Republican Parties."

Liberal fundamentalists argue that the party's presidential problems stem from insufficiently liberal Democratic candidates who have failed to rally the party's faithful. The facts, however, do not sustain this allegation.

[I]n the past two decades, liberalism has been transformed. The politics of innovation has been replaced by programmatic rigidity; the politics of inclusion has been superseded by ideological litmus tests. Worst of all, while insisting that they represent the popular will, contemporary liberals have lost touch with the American people. It is this transformed liberalism that we call "liberal fundamentalism," on which the electorate has rendered a series of negative judgments.

Liberal fundamentalism refuses to adjust to changing circumstances by adopting new means to achieve traditional ends. Instead, it enshrines the policies of the past two decades as sacrosanct and greets proposals for change with moral outrage. Whether the issue is the working poor, racial justice, educational excellence, or national defense, the liberal fundamentalist prescription is always the same; pursue the politics of the past. The result, predictably, has been programmatic stagnation and political defeat.

The authors bemoaned the party's weakness among young people:

The effects . . . are evident in two other ways: attitudes of young people towards the Republican Party, and the related erosion of Democratic strength among youth. According to ABC exit polls, Reagan won the 18-to 24-year-old age group by only one percentage point in 1980; four years later he won that same age group by 19 points. While less attractive to the youngest voters than Reagan, Bush still prevailed among them by five percentage points. By some measures, the tendency for the young to identify with the Republican Party is actually growing.

Galston and Kamarck summed up the Democratic Party predicament thus:

The inescapable fact is that the national Democratic Party is losing touch with the middle class, without whose solid support it cannot hope to rebuild a presidential majority.

Into this void strode Bill Clinton. While traditionally liberal in many of his beliefs, Clinton sent clear signals that he was a different kind of Democrat, not beholden to the liberal orthodoxies of the past. He said he wanted to "end welfare as we know it." He favored the death penalty, and approved executions as governor of Arkansas. He ripped into black rap singer Sister Souljah for her remark "If black people kill black people every day, why not have a week and kill white people?"[12] as filled with hatred and worthy of David Duke.

The result? In 1992, only three years after the Galston-Kamarck litany of Democratic woe, Bill Clinton was elected president of the United States. In the process, he transformed the Democratic Party and the future of American politics. He also demonstrated how quickly a troubled political party can solve its problems with the right candidate and the right message, and become a potent national political force once again.

A Worn-Out Business Model

From 1968 to 1988, Republicans offered the nation a winning business model that consistently sold effectively to a majority of the electorate as it was then constituted. The model appealed to young as well as old, northerners as well as southerners, Democrats as well as Republicans, and the middle class as well as the wealthy.

---

12. David Mills. "Sister Souljah's Call to Arms.' *Washington Post*, May 13, 1992, p. B1.

Unfortunately the old Republican business model is worn out at the presidential level. What once attracted overwhelming popular support no longer appeals to a majority of the national electorate as currently constituted. Fixing that worn-out business model is imperative for Republicans to become competitive at the presidential level once again.

Republicans need new messages, new messengers, and a new tone. It is not enough to say that Republicans need to communicate their existing message more effectively. Arguing that more effective communication alone will fix Republican problems is a fallacy that allows Republicans to avoid facing their more fundamental problems.

More effectively communicating unpopular ideas makes the problem worse, not better.

Republicans are making real progress in fixing the technological deficiencies so vividly exposed in the 2012 presidential campaign. The 2014 midterm results demonstrated that Republicans are beginning to catch up to the superb social networking, voter contact, and turnout machine the Democrats built around Barack Obama. But all the technological sophistication in the world will be for naught if, once they see it, voters are not willing to buy the product Republicans are selling.

Business men and women face these challenges all the time. The product that once sold beautifully now seems old and stale. A new competitor comes along with a superior version of the same product. A new product comes on the market that is so innovative it kills demand for an existing product—think cars and buggy whips in the last century, or streaming video and video tapes in this century.

Successful businesses anticipate the market of tomorrow. They listen to their customers and respond to changing needs and desires. Businesses that thrive in a fluid environment constantly change, adapt, and recalibrate. Those that don't, die.

Voters' preferences can help Republicans update their worn-out business model for the 21ˢᵗ century. Some components of the old business model can stay in an updated form, but others will have to go. That is the nature of an adaptive, innovative, and ultimately more competitive political party.

CHANGING DEMOGRAPHICS

Our grandfathers would never recognize the America of today, and our fathers are struggling to understand it. Demographic change has transformed the face of America and the composition of the American electorate so rapidly that it is difficult to comprehend.

The white population is barely growing at all, increasing by only 1 percent between 2000 and 2010. Because other racial groups are growing so much faster, whites[13] dropped from 69 percent of the U.S. population in 2000 to 64 percent only ten years later.[14] Whites now constitute a minority of the population in three states, including the mega-states of California and Texas. Our country will become a majority minority nation within the lifetimes of half the Americans who are alive today.

A new political message must sell well in the new America. Understanding that new America is critical for transforming the Republican Party.

Presidential Year Electorates

Changes in the presidential-year voting electorates reflect the rapidly changing demographics of the nation. Whites are declining as a proportion of the electorate at an increasing rate.

---

13. As in the previous chapter, "whites" refers to people who are not of Hispanic or Latino origin.

14. *http://www.census.gov/prod/cen2010/briefs/c2010br-05.pdf*

Racial Proportions in Presidential Electorates: 1976-2012

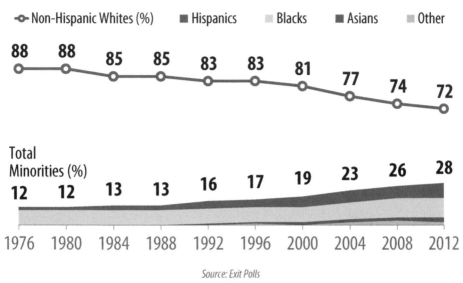

-o- Non-Hispanic Whites (%)   ■ Hispanics   ▨ Blacks   ■ Asians   ▨ Other

88   88   85   85   83   83   81   77   74   72

Total
Minorities (%)

12   12   13   13   16   17   19   23   26   28

1976   1980   1984   1988   1992   1996   2000   2004   2008   2012

Source: Exit Polls

Figure 2-1

Between 1976 and 1992, whites declined from 88 to 83 percent of the electorate. In other words, the proportion of whites declined by only 5 percentage points during the first sixteen years of this graph, from Jimmy Carter's election to Bill Clinton's first triumph. But during the second sixteen years from Clinton's reelection to Obama's reelection, the proportion of whites declined by 11 percentage points, more than twice the rate of decrease of the first period. By 2012 whites were down to 72 percent of the national electorate.

African-Americans remain the largest minority group among voters, but not for long. African-Americans constituted 10 percent of the electorate in 1976 and 13 percent in 2012. But their rate of growth pales in comparison to Hispanics and Asians. Hispanics grew from only 2 percent in 1976 to 10 percent in 2012. Asian turnout was so low it did not even rate a category in the exit polls of 1976. In 2012 Asians constituted 3 percent of the electorate nationally, and 11 percent of the crucial California electorate.[15]

The political changes driven by these shifting demographics constitute dramatic differences in the outcomes of elections, not just minor changes at the margins. If America had the same demographics in recent elections that it had when Ronald Reagan was elected president in 1980, John McCain would have won the presidency in 2008 and Mitt Romney would have been elected in 2012. Based on the way Barack Obama has governed, it is safe to say that changing demographics have already altered the course of the country.

Outlook for the 2016 Presidential Electorate

The trends outlined above show no sign of abating. In presidential electorates between 1996 and 2012, the proportion of whites declined and the proportion of non-whites increased from 2 to 4 percentage points every election. Taking the average—a 2.75-point decline in whites and a 2.75-point increase in non-whites—yields an estimate of the 2016 electorate of 69 percent white and 31 percent non-white.

Based on those white and non-white proportions of the 2016 presidential electorate, winning coalitions for the popular vote—those necessary to produce a total of 50.1 percent—look very different for the two political party nominees.

If the 2016 Republican nominee wins the same percentage of the white vote that Mitt Romney won in 2012—59 percent—then he or she will need to win 30 percent of the non-white vote to be elected. That is far greater than the 17 percent of the non-white vote that Romney achieved in 2012, or the 19 percent John McCain won in 2008, and better even

---

15. *http://elections.nbcnews.com/ns/politics/2012/california/president/#exitPoll*

than the 26 percent of the non-white vote that George W. Bush won in his 2004 reelection campaign.

On the other hand, if the 2016 Republican nominee wins no more of the non-white vote than Romney's 17 percent, he or she will need to win 65 percent of the white vote to win. That is a level of white vote achieved by only one Republican nominee in the past forty years: Ronald Reagan in his 49-state landslide reelection sweep in 1984, when he won 66 percent of the white vote.

The challenge for Republicans is obvious. Even George W. Bush's comfortable reelection win in 2004, with 58 percent of the white vote and 26 percent of the non-white vote, would be a losing hand in 2016.

Republican Winning Coalition in the Likely 2016 Presidential Electorate

	Whites	Non-Whites
2016 scenarios	59%	30%
	60%	28%
	61%	26%
	62%	24%
	63%	21%
	64%	19%
	65%	17%
Romney 2012	59%	17%
McCain 2008	55%	19%
Bush 2004	58%	26%

Figure 2-2

The Democratic winning coalition looks very different. Barack Obama won 39 percent of the white vote and 82 percent of the non-white vote on the way to his 51.1 percent victory in 2012. If the Democratic nominee in 2016 wins the same 39 percent of the white vote as Obama, he or she could win the presidency by gaining 75 percent of the non-white vote.

At this writing, Hillary Clinton looks like the odds-on favorite to win the Democratic nomination in 2016. In her 2008 primary campaign she was a far more attractive candidate than Obama among whites who voted in Democratic primaries, especially in poorer regions of the country like Appalachia. If she is able to push her percentage among whites up to 42 percent, then she needs only 68 percent of the non-white vote to win the presidency. That is far lower than the 82 percent of the non-white vote Obama achieved in 2012, the 81 percent he won in 2008, or even the 73 percent John Kerry won in 2004.

Democratic Winning Coalition in the Likely 2016 Presidential Electorate

	Whites	Non-Whites
2016 scenarios	38%	77%
	39%	75%
	40%	73%
	41%	70%
	42%	68%
Obama 2012	39%	82%
Obama 2008	43%	81%
Kerry 2004	41%	73%

Figure 2-3

Non-Presidential Year Electorates

The white proportion of midterm electorates has historically been larger than in presidential years. While exit polls do not go back as far in midterm as presidential years, the following chart shows exactly the same trend. This is one reason why Republicans tend to perform better in off-years like 2010 and 2014. But time is running out for a party overwhelmingly reliant on white voters, even in midterm elections.

Racial Proportions in Midterm Electorates: 1994-2014

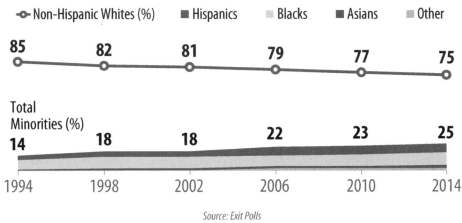

Source: Exit Polls

Figure 2–4

Demographic Trends in the Population by Age Group

The proportion of minority groups among people who actually vote in elections lag behind their proportion in the population at large. That is partly because new immigrants are less likely to register to vote, and partly because so many members of minority groups are too young to vote. But trends in the broader population foreshadow the makeup of future electorates as new immigrants register to vote and young people reach voting age.

The following chart shows the American population by age groups in 2015. Other than children who will be born in 2015, all of these people are already living in America.

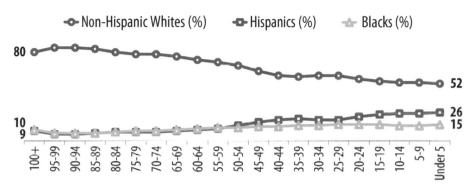

Racial Proportions in Five-Year Age Cohorts in 2015

Source: U.S. Census Bureau Table 6, Released December 2012

Figure 2-5

Among seniors who will be 65 and older in 2015, whites range from 76 to 84 percent of each five-year age group. White dominance of older age groups is one reason why Republicans have performed relatively better among seniors than among younger groups in the last two presidential elections.

Among middle-aged Americans, the proportion of whites declines from 73 percent of people age 60 to 64 down to 58 percent of those 35 to 39 years old. In every single five-year age cohort, the proportion of whites is smaller than the last.

Among young people age 20 to 34, the proportion of whites ranges from 59 percent down to 56 percent. But it is among Americans under age 20 that the demographic changes are most dramatic. The proportion of whites ranges from 54 percent among those 15 to 19 years old down to 52 percent among children under age 5.

African-Americans constitute a larger share of young people than the elderly. Among seniors, blacks make up 9 percent of the population and about 12 percent of those middle-aged. Among young adults and children, blacks constitute about 14 percent of the population.

The fastest growing ethnic group in the population in percentage terms is not Hispanics but Asians. Asians constitute about 4 percent of American seniors and about 5 percent of Americans under age 65. Asians have become very important politically in selected states, notably California and Virginia. Their rapid growth rate is driven more by the small base from which they started than by their absolute numbers nationally. Between 2000 and 2010 Asians grew by 43.3 percent to a total of 14.7 million.[16]

It is among Hispanics where the population growth among young people is most dramatic. Hispanics, who make up only 8 percent of seniors and 12 percent of those age 50 to 64, constitute 19 percent of Americans age 20 to 49 and fully 25 percent of teenagers and children. In every single five-year age cohort below age 35, Hispanics constitute a larger and larger percentage of Americans.

The political implications are hard to overestimate. Every single month for the next two decades, 50,000 Hispanic youngsters will turn 18 years old and become eligible to vote.[17] Any political party that hopes to win national elections in the 21st century must be competitive among Hispanic Americans.

Long-Term Demographic Trends

The U.S. Census Bureau projects the following demographic trends over the next half century and paints a picture of how America will change by the year 2060. The following chart shows the dramatic result.

---

16. U.S. Census Bureau Table 1, Population by Hispanic or Latino Origin and by Race for the United States: 2000 and 2010

17. *http://www.hispanicvoters2012.com*

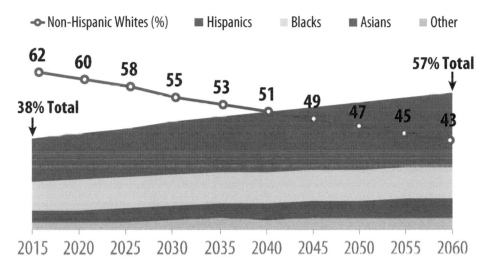

Census Projections of Racial Proportions in the Population: 2015-2060

-○- Non-Hispanic Whites (%)   ▪ Hispanics   ▪ Blacks   ▪ Asians   ▪ Other

62   60   58   55   53   51   49   47   45   43

57% Total

38% Total

2015 2020 2025 2030 2035 2040 2045 2050 2055 2060

Source: U.S. Census Bureau Table 6, Released December 2012

Figure 2-6

White Americans, who have constituted a majority of the American population since the Declaration of Independence, will no longer do so by 2045. In absolute numbers they are barely growing at all. Because minority groups are growing so much faster, whites are rapidly declining as a share of the population. By 2060 whites will make up only 43 percent of the American population, with various other minority ethnic groups making up 57 percent.

African-Americans, long the nation's largest minority group, will hardly grow at all as a percentage of the country's population, moving from 12 percent in 2015 to 13 percent in 2060.

The number of Asians will grow by almost 50 percent in absolute numbers by 2060, but as a share of the country's population they will increase only from 5 to 8 percent.

The greatest increase, of course, will occur among Hispanics. At 16 percent they are already the nation's largest ethnic minority group in terms of population. By 2020 they will make up 19 percent of the country's population. Every decade thereafter they will grow by an additional 3 percentage points, so that by 2030 they will constitute 22 percent of the population, 25 percent by 2040, 28 percent by 2050, and 31 percent by 2060.

At 43 percent of the population, whites will still be more numerous than Hispanics by 2060. But with whites declining by 4 percentage points a decade, and Hispanics growing by 3 points a decade, if those trends continue the number of Hispanics will surpass whites about 2080.

Other races—Native Americans, Pacific Islanders, and people of multiple races will make up the remainder of the American population.

Critics can argue that the Census Bureau exaggerates these changes. But even if the critics are right, only the slope of the lines in the chart will change, not the overall picture.

Conclusion

Republicans can complain about these trends, wring their hands over them, and get heartburn as a result. What they can't do is change them. Broad demographic change in the American electorate is inexorable and irreversible. The only rational response to these trends is to recognize them, plan for them, and figure out how to succeed with them. The political party that best anticipates and plans for the new America will own the future.

Republicans can not only survive, but thrive in the 21st century. Republican values of individual liberty, free enterprise, limited government, and expanded opportunity for all know no ethnic boundaries. Just as successive waves of immigrants have before them, Hispanic and Asian Americans respond to the incentives and opportunities offered by this amazing land. Republican candidates can win a far higher share of minority votes than they have in recent elections with a better message and aggressive efforts to appeal to the new America that is rapidly approaching.

★ ★ ★ 3 ★ ★ ★

THE ROLE *of* GOVERNMENT

Disagreement about the proper role of government in the economic life of a nation has long defined differences between the Democratic and Republican parties. Far more than differences on education or health care or taxes or any other particular issue, getting the role of government right is foundational for a political party searching for a new direction and a new message. Does the current philosophy of government held by the Republican Party resonate with the 21ˢᵗ century presidential electorate?

Republicans have long comforted themselves in the wake of Democratic presidential victories with the belief that America remains a center-right country. Over time, the argument goes, the center-right party will reassert its dominance over the center-left party once we get beyond the weaknesses of various candidates or the short-term negative effects of recessions or unpopular wars.

Yet the surge in racial minorities in the electorate, especially in presidential election years, and the reelection of Barack Obama in 2012 during a weak economy, raises a fundamental question: is America still a center-right country? Or have demographic changes and economic angst shifted the American ideological mean to the left? Are we now more like western Europe in our values? Have we now become a center-left rather than a center-right country for presidential elections?

For the better part of the last decade, jobs and the economy have topped the list of most important issues to American voters. Economic angst is palpable and obvious to anyone who has watched a focus group discuss our economic future. Sluggish job growth during the past two economic recoveries has cast doubt on the capability of our economy to generate the kinds of economic opportunities we took for granted in the latter half of the 20ᵗʰ century. The pressures of globalization have caused many Americans to wonder if the era of American world economic dominance is over.

Economic weakness has given the American left the rationale to argue for a vast expansion of federal government spending, regardless of the consequences for our long-term fiscal health. But our economy has seemed immune to even trillion-dollar stimulus packages like Barack Obama's 2009 spending spree. The response from the left? Spend even more money. Grow the federal government ever larger. Bankrupt the country in order to save it.

Obama's 2012 reelection in the face of such fruitless fiscal profligacy raises legitimate questions about whether America remains a center-right country.

What Does Center-Right Mean?

While we may quibble about the relative weight given to each component, the center-right governing philosophy is rooted in a set of values widely shared across the center-right coalition:

- Individual liberty as the cornerstone of the American experiment.

- The Constitution as the foundation for our government and our liberties.

- Free enterprise as the primary engine of economic growth.

- Individual initiative and entrepreneurial endeavor as the driving forces behind societal advancement.

- Limited government that regulates excesses of free markets and provides a safety net for those undergoing hard times, but otherwise allows individual liberty and initiative to flourish.

- Personal responsibility as the flip side of limited government, where individuals look to themselves first to solve problems, only looking to government after their individual efforts and non-governmental institutions have been unsuccessful.

- Equality of opportunity, defined as creating a level playing field for economic competition, coupled with opposition to redistributing the resulting unequal outcomes.

- Lower taxes to allow people to keep more of the fruits of their labors.

- The family as the basic building block of a healthy society.

- Strong national defense and leadership in the world as befits the world's only remaining superpower.

- American exceptionalism as the animating belief that America remains the most unique and exciting political and economic experiment in the history of the world.

Have these values become passé? Are we now irreversibly addicted to larger and larger government? Do we now look to a paternalistic government as the primary source of our well-being and security? Are we well on our way to becoming a European-style social welfare state?

You would think the answer to all of those questions is "yes" based upon the Obama campaign's Life of Julia, a cartoon offering the left's vision for a new government-centered utopia. Julia, created during Obama's run for reelection in 2012, was fortunate enough to live in the new Obama-created America where she could rely on cradle-to-grave government support and a long life of dependence on government.[18]

---

18. *http://fortmchenry.tumblr.com/post/80091170280/lifeofjulia*

The Life of Julia

- At age 3 Julia is enrolled in the federally-funded Head Start program to help get her ready for school.

- At 17 Julia's high school is part of the federal Race to the Top program implemented by President Obama to set new federal college and career- ready standards.

- At 18 Julia and her family qualify for President Obama's American Opportunity Tax Credit. She also receives a federal Pell Grant to help her afford college.

- At 22 Julia has surgery that is covered by her parents' health insurance policy because of ObamaCare regulations.

- At 23 Julia starts her career as a web designer knowing she will get equal pay because of the Obama-supported Lilly Ledbetter Fair Pay Act.

- At 25 Julia can pay back her student loans more easily because President Obama capped student loan payments and kept interest rates low.

- At 27 Julia gets her birth control and preventive care covered by her insurance company because of ObamaCare regulations.

- At 31 Julia decides to have a child (sans husband), and because of ObamaCare she gets free screenings, maternal checkups, and prenatal care.

- At 37 Julia's son Zachary starts kindergarten in a public school that has better facilities and great teachers because of President Obama's federal spending on education and programs like the federal Race to the Top.

- At 42 Julia starts her own web design business with a federally-funded small business loan.

- At 65 Julia enrolls in the federally-funded Medicare program.

- At 67 Julia retires and lives comfortably off her federal Social Security payments that allow her to volunteer at a community garden.

How could Julia possibly get through life without the all-caring, all-knowing, always supportive federal government? Paternalistic government is fundamental and indispensable for Julia throughout her entire time on this earth.

Though widely mocked by conservatives,[19] the Obama campaign never disavowed the cartoon, perhaps because it accurately captured the liberal vision for America.

Julia's life is the antithesis of a self-reliant individual who looks first to herself, her family, her church, her community, and her job for her well-being, relying on government only as a last resort during particularly tough times.

Is this what America has become? If Julia is now the dominant role model for a great American life, a center-right party has little hope of commanding a majority of the electorate. Fortunately for Republicans, a mountain of public opinion data indicates that the answer to that question is "no."

Ideology of the American Electorate

First, based on their self-identified ideology in presidential election years, no evidence suggests that the American electorate has become substantially more liberal over the last thirty-two years. In 1980, 31 percent of those who voted for Ronald Reagan considered themselves to be conservative; in 2012 the electorate that voted for Barack Obama contained even more self-identified conservatives, 35 percent. Liberals have grown some-

---

19. A couple of great examples are here: *http://www.youtube.com/watch?v=F5xaZB8AgAQ* and *http://thelifeofjulia.com*

what over those thirty-two years, rising from 18 percent in 1980 to 25 percent in 2012. But even with that growth, conservatives still outnumber liberals by 10 percentage points in the electorate that reelected Obama.

Ideological Distribution of Presidential Electorates: 1980-2012

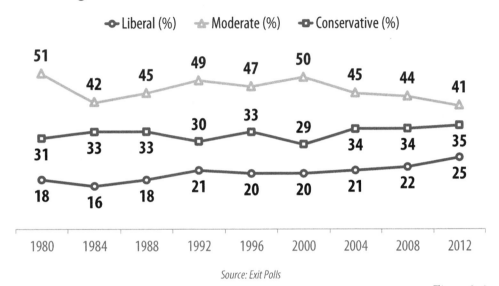

Source: Exit Polls

Figure 3–1

In the fall of 2013, our firm asked adults to place themselves on a 7-point ideological scale, with 1 as "very liberal" and 7 as "very conservative." Those results show the mean for the entire electorate standing at 4.47, just to the right of center. As with the ideological makeup of the presidential electorates for the past thirty-two years, American adults remain center-right on the ideological scale.

Ideological Means of Democrats, Republicans, and All Voters in 2013

"When thinking about politics today, do you normally consider yourself to be very conservative, somewhat conservative, moderate, somewhat liberal, or very liberal? [IF MODERATE, ASK:] Do you lean toward being liberal or conservative?"

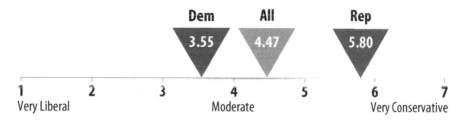

Source: *Bipartisan Policy Center/USA Today /North Star Opinion Research, National Survey of Adults, September 19-23, 2013*

Figure 3-2

That survey also shows, however, that the Republican mean of 5.80 is farther from both the absolute center (4.0), and the mean of the entire electorate (4.47), than the Democratic mean of 3.55. Having Republicans stand farther from the rest of the electorate than Democrats creates challenges that will be explored in subsequent chapters.

Maybe self-described ideology no longer reflects peoples' actual policy preferences? Maybe conservatives are as hooked on government as everyone else? Perhaps the large cadre of "moderates"—41 percent of the 2012 electorate—are really liberals who don't want to admit it? As we will see, precious little evidence exists to support any of those propositions.

Attitudes About the Federal Government

Part of the problem for liberals in promoting their desire for larger government is widespread disgust with the federal government. While Congress has not been held in particularly high esteem for years—the only time a substantial majority approved of congressional job performance during the past forty years was immediately after 9/11—it at least managed to gain approval from a quarter to a third of Americans during most of that period. But as partisanship increased and gridlock ensued during the Obama years, congressional job approval sank to abysmally low levels. Americans are unwilling to give more power and authority to a Congress they detest.

Congressional Job Approval: 1974-2015

"Do you approve or disapprove of the way Congress is handling its job?"

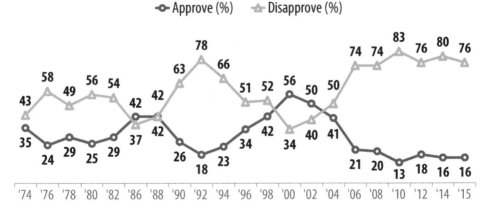

Source: Gallup data from surveys taken 1974-2015. Copyright 2015 Gallup, Inc. All rights reserved.

Figure 3-3

While not as negative as attitudes toward Congress, Americans' views of the rest of the federal government are hardly stellar. A majority—52 percent—thinks the federal government has a mainly negative impact on their lives, with 43 percent saying it has a positive impact. A similar majority—55 percent—gives the federal government a rating of C or D or F, while only a quarter give it an A or B.[20]

The same proportion—55 percent—think they get less value out of what the federal government does for them than they pay in taxes; only 7 percent say they get more value than they pay (the remainder think they get about the right amount of value). Interestingly, the inveterate optimism of the American people remains intact—fully 79 percent of Americans believe "it is possible for the federal government to be run well," while only 20 percent disagree.[21] The problem is that they do not think it is being run well now.

Why would Americans want to give the federal government more authority over their lives when eight out of ten disapprove of Congress, when a majority thinks the government has a negative impact on their lives, when they give the government a C, D, or F rating for its performance, and when they do not think they are getting value for their money? The answer is that they don't.

Government Size, Services, and Taxes

When asked about the size of government, coupled with the requirement to pay for whatever government we get, overwhelming majorities of Americans consistently prefer a smaller government with fewer services and lower taxes to a larger government with more services and higher taxes. Even Democratic voters prefer smaller government when coupled with the requirement to pay for it.

---

20. *http://kaiserfamilyfoundation.files.wordpress.com/2013/01/8112.pdf*

21. Ibid

Smaller Government/Lower Taxes or Larger Government/Higher Taxes by Political Party

"Overall, would you prefer smaller government with fewer services and lower taxes, or larger government with more services and higher taxes?"

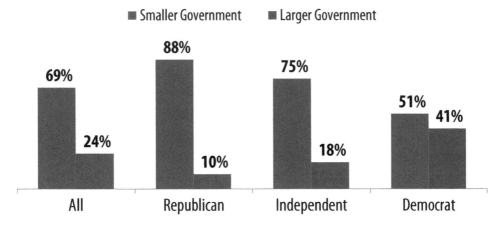

Source: Crossroads GPS/North Star Opinion Research, National Survey of Registered Voters, June 2-5, 2013

Figure 3-4

Self-described "moderates" are hardly apostles for larger government. While they fall between conservatives and liberals on this question, they are far closer to the conservative than the liberal end of the spectrum.

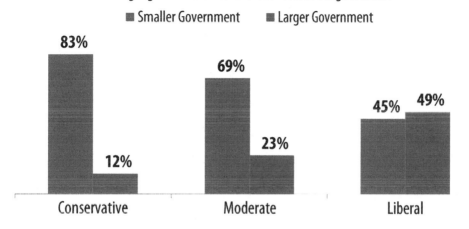

Smaller Government/Lower Taxes or Larger Government/Higher Taxes by Ideology

"Overall, would you prefer smaller government with fewer services and lower taxes, or larger government with more services and higher taxes?"

■ Smaller Government   ■ Larger Government

Conservative: 83% / 12%
Moderate: 69% / 23%
Liberal: 45% / 49%

Source: Crossroads GPS/North Star Opinion Research, National Survey of Registered Voters, June 2-5, 2013

Figure 3-5

Nor has that result changed significantly over the course of Obama's presidency. Preference for a smaller government with fewer services and lower taxes is identical to where it stood in April of 2009 at 69 percent. Those favoring a larger government with more services and higher taxes have inched up 3 percentage points from 21 to 24 percent, but still trail far behind the preference for smaller government.

Change Among All Voters: Smaller Government/Lower Taxes or Larger Government/Higher Taxes: 2009-2013

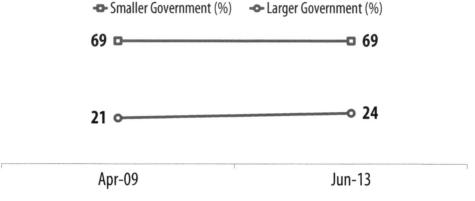

"Overall, would you prefer smaller government with fewer services and lower taxes, or larger government with more services and higher taxes?"

Sources: Resurgent Republic/North Star Opinion Research, April 2009, Crossroads GPS/North Star Opinion Research, June 2013

Figure 3-6

The key phrase driving this outcome is "higher taxes." Asking this question without taxes still produces a preference for smaller government, but by a narrower margin. And why wouldn't it? We all like stuff someone else is paying for. But a majority still prefers smaller government.

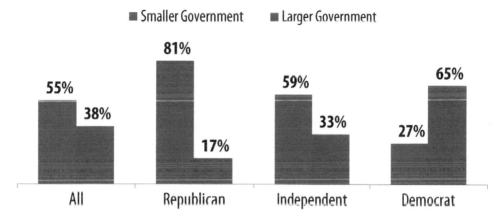

Smaller Government/Fewer Services or Larger Government/More Services by Political Party

"Overall, would you prefer smaller government with fewer services, or larger government with more services?"

■ Smaller Government   ■ Larger Government

	Smaller	Larger
All	55%	38%
Republican	81%	17%
Independent	59%	33%
Democrat	27%	65%

Source: Crossroads GPS/North Star Opinion Research, National Survey of Registered Voters, June 2-5, 2013

Figure 3-7

The same pattern occurs by ideology, with conservatives and moderates preferring smaller government with fewer services to a larger government with more services.

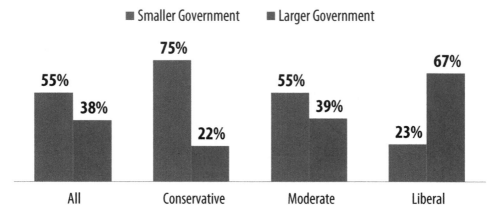

Smaller Government/Fewer Services or Larger Government/More Services by Ideology

"Overall, would you prefer smaller government with fewer services, or larger government with more services?"

■ Smaller Government   ■ Larger Government

Source: Crossroads GPS/North Star Opinion Research, National Survey of Registered Voters, June 2-5, 2013

Figure 3-8

Interestingly, the groups that shift the most on the question that removes the requirement to pay for more services are Democrats and liberals. They are all for larger government with more services as long as someone else pays for them. But adding the requirement of "higher taxes" to pay for that larger government makes even a majority of Democrats want smaller government and lower taxes!

Using a similarly worded question, Gallup shows the preference for "more services if that meant more taxes" remaining constant over the past two decades at 20 percent. The desire for "less government services in order to reduce taxes" grew from 40 to 47 percent.

Change Among All Voters: Less Government to Reduce Taxes: 1993-2013

"Would you rather have more government services if that meant more taxes, less services in order to reduce taxes, or services and taxes about as we have them now?"

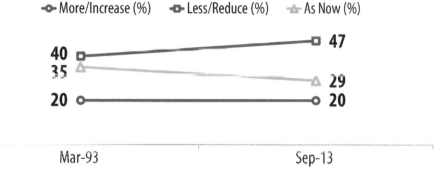

Source: Gallup, March 22-24, 1993 and September 5-8, 2013. Copyright 2015 Gallup, Inc. All rights reserved.

Figure 3-9

Differently worded questions that eliminate the reference to taxes still do not produce a preference for larger government. In 2010 Gallup asked respondents to place themselves on a 1-to-5 scale with 1 being "the government should do only those things necessary to provide the most basic government functions, and 5 means you think the government should take active steps in every area it can to try and improve the lives of its citizens." The overall response ended up dead in the center of the scale, with one-third choosing 1 or 2, one-third saying 3, and one-third picking 4 or 5. But Independents leaned to the "just basic government functions" end of the scale by 35 to 28 percent.

Government Activity Scale by Political Party

"Next, I'd like you to think more broadly about the purposes of government. Where would you rate yourself on a scale of 1 to 5, where 1 means you think the government should do only those things necessary to provide the most basic government functions, and 5 means you think the government should take active steps in every area it can to try and improve the lives of its citizens?"

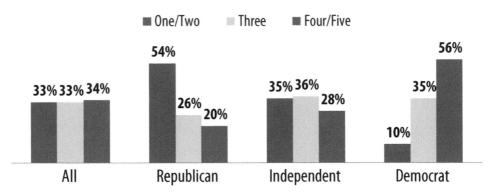

Figure 3–10

Using still different wording on how much government is trying to do, Gallup finds a majority of the country consistently believing that "the government is trying to do too many things that should be left to individuals and businesses" rather than the "government should do more to solve our country's problems." A temporary aberration occurred right after the terrorist attacks on 9/11 when people wanted the government to do more, but the numbers quickly reverted to a baseline of believing that the government is trying to do too much by a double-digit margin.[(22)]

When asked about the size of government, the willingness to pay for more services, or the desire for more government to "solve our country's problems," there is simply no evidence that America has shifted to the left. On the appropriate role of government, America remains a center-right country in presidential election years.

22. *http://www.gallup.com/poll/164444/americans-remain-divided-role-gov-play.aspx*

Income Redistribution

So if Americans do not want a larger government with more services and higher taxes, how about governmental efforts to redistribute income to reduce income inequality? Doesn't everyone want more equality? Don't we all value "fairness?" Not if it comes at the cost of our entrepreneurial spirit and allowing people to keep more of what they earn.

When faced with a choice of government policies promoting "fairness by narrowing the gap between rich and poor, making the rich pay their fair share, and reducing income inequality" on the one hand, and government policies promoting "opportunity by fostering job growth, encouraging entrepreneurs, and allowing hardworking people to keep more of what they earn" on the other, opportunity wins hands down. Republicans and Independents choose opportunity overwhelmingly. Democrats prefer fairness, but the margin is relatively close, with nearly one-third of Democrats still picking opportunity.

Opportunity versus Inequality by Political Party

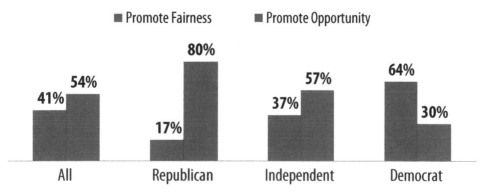

"Which of the following statements comes closer to your view: **A)** Government policies should promote fairness by narrowing the gap between rich and poor, making the rich pay their fair share, and reducing income inequality; **B)** Government policies should promote opportunity by fostering job growth, encouraging entrepreneurs, and allowing hardworking people to keep more of what they earn."

■ Promote Fairness   ■ Promote Opportunity

	All	Republican	Independent	Democrat
Promote Fairness	41%	17%	37%	64%
Promote Opportunity	54%	80%	57%	30%

Source: Resurgent Republic/North Star Opinion Research,

Figure 3-11

50

Barack Obama's constant refrain as president of "making the rich pay their fair share" has narrowed the gap on the question, primarily by moving Democrats from an even split in 2009 to a substantial preference for "fairness" by 2012.

Opportunity versus Inequality among Democrats: 2009-2012

"Which of the following statements comes closer to your view: **A)** Government policies should promote fairness by narrowing the gap between rich and poor, making the rich pay their fair share, and reducing income inequality; **B)** Government policies should promote opportunity by fostering job growth, encouraging entrepreneurs, and allowing hardworking people to keep more of what they earn."

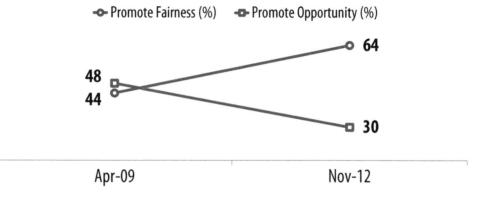

Sources: Resurgent Republic/North Star Opinion Research, National Surveys

Figure 3–12

Independents shifted more modestly in the same direction during Obama's first term, but still favor opportunity over fairness.

Opportunity versus Inequality among Independents: 2009-2012

"Which of the following statements comes closer to your view: **A)** Government policies should promote fairness by narrowing the gap between rich and poor, making the rich pay their fair share, and reducing income inequality; **B)** Government policies should promote opportunity by fostering job growth, encouraging entrepreneurs, and allowing hardworking people to keep more of what they earn."

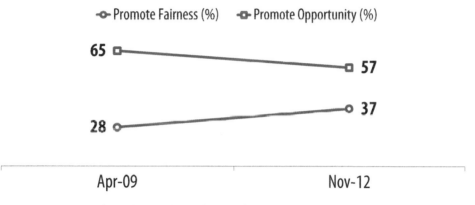

Sources: Resurgent Republic/North Star Opinion Research, National Surveys

Figure 3-13

Republicans actually increased their overwhelming preference for opportunity during Obama's first term, probably reacting against Obama's drumbeat for more "fairness."

Opportunity versus Inequality among Republicans: 2009-2012

"Which of the following statements comes closer to your view: **A)** Government policies should promote fairness by narrowing the gap between rich and poor, making the rich pay their fair share, and reducing income inequality; **B)** Government policies should promote opportunity by fostering job growth, encouraging entrepreneurs, and allowing hardworking people to keep more of what they earn."

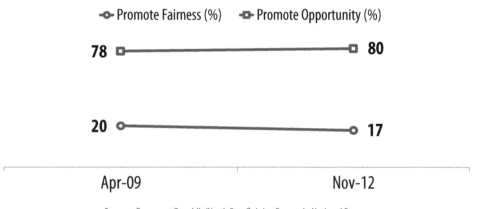

Promote Fairness (%) Promote Opportunity (%)

78 ▭——————————————————▭ 80

20 ○——————————————————○ 17

Apr-09   Nov-12

Sources: Resurgent Republic/North Star Opinion Research, National Surveys

Figure 3-14

In 2013 President Obama argued that growing income inequality is "the defining challenge of our time."[23] But most Americans simply do not agree. Fewer than half of Americans say the gap between the rich and poor is a very big problem, far fewer than those who identify inequality as a major concern in other advanced countries.[24] And only about one-

23. *http://www.usatoday.com/story/news/politics/2013/12/04/obama-income-inequality-speech-center-for-american-progress/3867747/*

24. *http://www.pewresearch.org/fact-tank/2013/12/06/the-u-s-s-high-income-gap-is-met-with-relatively-low-public-concern/*

sixth of Americans want inequality to be the government's top economic concern.[25]

Americans overwhelmingly want a chance to succeed, an opportunity to work hard, and an ability to keep more of the fruits of their labors. They want an equal opportunity to grow and develop and use their skills. They do *not* want a government that mandates equal outcomes, that redistributes income, and that promotes a liberal vision of "fairness." That sounds suspiciously like a center-right perspective on our economic life.

Conclusion

On the defining issue of the philosophy and role of government, America remains a center-right country. Support for the center-right values of individual liberty, free enterprise, limited government, personal responsibility, and expanded opportunity remains robust in the American electorate of the 21st century.

With the right candidate, the right message, and the right tone, the center-right party should be able to win a presidential election in a center-right country.

---

25. *http://www.pewresearch.org/fact-tank/2013/12/26/6-global-challenges-for-2014/*

★ ★ ★ 4 ★ ★ ★

TAXES, SPENDING, DEFICITS, *and* DEBT

Other than ObamaCare, no issue has dominated national political dis-
course during the Obama presidency more than taxes, spending, deficits,
and debt. Washington's inability to reach anything close to a consensus on
fiscal issues has caused the government to lurch from crisis to crisis, from
one continuing resolution to the next, looking utterly dysfunctional in the
process. Probably no other issue has driven congressional approval ratings
into the gutter more than the inability to resolve the most fundamental
fiscal questions of governance: how much are we going to tax, and how
much are we going to spend?

What guidance can public opinion offer on the way out of this mess? How
can Republicans craft a fiscal message that will appeal to a majority of
the 21st century presidential electorate? Can any approach garner popular
support in this ideologically riven country?

Let's begin by acknowledging a few realities. First, American voters are
not experts on the federal budget. Many Americans believe things about
the federal budget that are just not so:

- That foreign aid constitutes at least one-fourth of federal
  spending (the reality is about one percent).[26]

- That the budget can be balanced without touching entitlement
  programs (Social Security, Medicare, Medicaid, unemployment,

---

26. *http://www.washingtonpost.com/blogs/wonkblog/wp/2013/11/07/the-budget-
myth-that-just-wont-die-americans-still-think-28-percent-of-the-budget-goes-to-
foreign-aid/*

food stamps, and other entitlement programs constitute 62 percent of the federal budget).[27]

- That defense spending eats up the bulk of the federal budget (defense spending as a proportion of the budget—currently about 19 percent—has been in a long decline since the Korean War in the early 1950s).

- That the budget can be balanced by eliminating ubiquitous "waste, fraud, and abuse." Leaving aside the inconvenient point that one person's "critically necessary program" is another person's "waste, fraud, and abuse," voters continually tell pollsters that waste, fraud, and abuse is the real reason why the budget cannot be balanced.

Second, public opinion polling can demonstrate support for almost any budgetary decision in isolation. Large majorities can be generated to support almost any spending program in the federal budget—why would we not support more services or higher benefits divorced from their cost? Similar majorities can be created to oppose almost any tax increase—why would we support more money coming out of our pockets if the budget could be balanced by eliminating "waste, fraud, and abuse?"

---

27. *http://s3.amazonaws.com/resurgentrepublic.com/resurgentrepublic/production/assets/428/original/RR_August_Toplines.pdf*

Opposition to Various Federal Tax Increases

"Now I'm going to read a list of federal income tax changes that are scheduled to occur on January 1, 2011. For each one, please tell me if you support or oppose that change:"

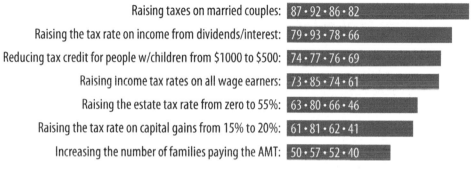

Ranked by Percent "Oppose"— All · Rep · Ind · Dem

Raising taxes on married couples: 87 · 92 · 86 · 82

Raising the tax rate on income from dividends/interest: 79 · 93 · 78 · 66

Reducing tax credit for people w/children from $1000 to $500: 74 · 77 · 76 · 69

Raising income tax rates on all wage earners: 73 · 85 · 74 · 61

Raising the estate tax rate from zero to 55%: 63 · 80 · 66 · 46

Raising the tax rate on capital gains from 15% to 20%: 61 · 81 · 62 · 41

Increasing the number of families paying the AMT: 50 · 57 · 52 · 40

Source: Resurgent Republic / North Star Opinion Research,
Survey of Likely Voters in Senate Battleground States, July 17-20, 2010

Figure 4-1

Fiscal decisions are inherently about trade-offs, about whether this program is more important than that one, about whether this new spending idea is worth raising that tax to pay for it, about whether the negative economic impact of raising that tax will be greater or worse than the revenue generated.

Public opinion questions that are most useful on fiscal matters pose those trade-offs, and force respondents to make the same kinds of difficult choices as those facing elected officials.

Do Deficits Really Matter?

The overarching question when addressing taxes and spending is whether deficits really matter at all. Economists engage in raging debates about the effect of deficits on the economy, but the question here is whether they matter politically. Does running up large deficits have any political consequence? Does any significant portion of the electorate vote based on

58

the size of the deficit, rewarding elected officials who reduce the deficit and punishing those who expand it? Do presidents who preside over large deficits have difficulty getting reelected?

Based on the evidence of the past half-century, the answer appears to be "no" to each of those questions. Consider the following chart:

Size of the Deficit or Surplus: 1968-2014

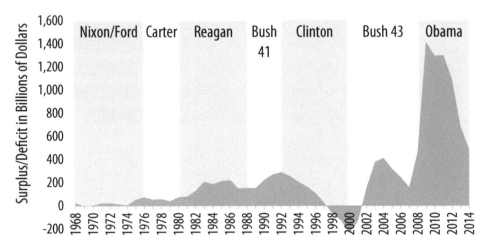

Source: Office of Management and Budget, Historical Tables, Table 1.1

Figure 4-2

During the early years of this chart, Richard Nixon won in 1972 when the deficit stood at a paltry $23 billion, Gerald Ford lost in 1976 when the deficit was $73 billion, and Jimmy Carter lost in 1980 when the deficit was essentially unchanged at $74 billion. It is hard to argue that the deficit had any effect whatsoever on these three outcomes.

How about the next dozen years when deficits started to grow? Ronald Reagan presided over the largest deficit increase in American history other than World War II, from $74 billion to $185 billion, yet he was reelected in a 49-state landslide. The deficit declined only slightly down to $155 billion when his vice president George H. W. Bush was comfortably elected in 1988. The deficit jumped up to $269 billion in 1992 when Bush lost reelection, but most political observers attribute that loss to the economic recession that helped drive up the deficit rather than the deficit itself.

Do presidents get any credit for reducing the deficit? During Bill Clinton's administration the deficit plunged from $290 billion down to $107 billion during his first term leading to his comfortable reelection, and then further down below zero to a $236 billion *surplus* by the time he left office. Yet his vice president Al Gore was unable to win a majority of Electoral College votes in 2000.

During George W. Bush's first term the deficit climbed in the wake of 9/11 from a $236 billion surplus to a $413 billion deficit, a $649 billion turnaround. Yet Bush was still able to defeat John Kerry in his reelection campaign in 2004. From there the deficit increased somewhat to $459 billion in 2008 when John McCain lost to Barack Obama.

Then the wheels came off. In Barack Obama's first year the deficit grew from $459 billion up to $1.423 trillion, a breathtaking jump of $964 billion in one year alone. The deficit each of the next three years was $1.294 trillion, $1.3 trillion, and $1.087 trillion. Yet Barack Obama won a comfortable reelection in 2012.

How can we look at that record and argue that deficits matter in the least? We can make the case that deficits contributed to the Tea Party-driven Republican takeover of the House of Representatives in 2010. But when the president who presided over such dramatic increases in the deficit wins reelection, are they really relevant at all?

Is it any wonder that Dick Cheney famously argued, "Reagan proved that deficits don't matter." Newt Gingrich ripped Bob Dole as "tax collector for the welfare state" for his desire to ensure that revenues and expenditures come close to balance. Others called those arguing for fiscal responsibility "green eye shade Republicans," mocking them as narrow-minded bean counters who lacked any larger vision about where to take the country or how to make the economy grow.

The appropriate Republican goal, these leaders argued, should be to "starve the beast," limiting tax revenue to put a brake on Democratic spending and the growth of government. Implicitly acknowledging Republican inability to stop or control the Democrats' spending impulses, this line of reasoning suggests that controlling spending can only be done by limiting revenue.

But it has not worked out that way. The first term of the Obama administration and Democratic majorities of Congress demonstrated that they are not in the least constrained by the amount of revenue available. Consequently spending in recent years soared as a percentage of the Gross Domestic Product to levels not seen since World War II.

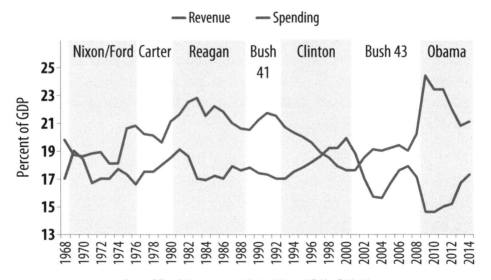

Source: Office of Management and Budget, Historical Tables, Table 1.2

Figure 4–3

So, limiting revenue constitutes no constraint on out-of-control spending. Consequently the nation faces enormous deficits as far as the eye can see. Even though the deficit for 2014 was significantly lower than the prior five years, that is only a temporary respite before the baby boomer generation retires and begins drawing Social Security and Medicare benefits.

Perhaps the critics are right. Maybe there is no market in today's America for a politician who believes that our enormous deficits and the resulting mountain of debt are economically perilous for the citizens of today and morally irresponsible for those of tomorrow. Maybe the political benefits flow only to those on the left who want to increase spending without regard to revenues and those on the right who want to cut taxes without regard to spending. Indeed, all the incentives in our democratic political system appear to lead directly away from fiscally responsible outcomes.

The Tragedy of the Fiscal Commons

In the Tragedy of the Commons, the economists' famous metaphor based on a 1968 essay by ecologist Garrett Hardin in the journal *Science*,[28] a group of herders shares a common pasture for grazing their cows. Each herder has an incentive to increase the number of cows he sends to the pasture, even though if all herders follow the same incentive the pasture will be destroyed by overgrazing. A herder receives all the benefits of grazing an additional animal, but the costs of overgrazing are borne by the entire group. Moreover, the benefit received by the herder comes relatively quickly by gaining another animal to take to market, but the cost comes in the longer term by destroying the pasture.

Economists typically have applied this example to population growth, or environmental problems like overfishing, where individuals behaving rationally in their own self-interest destroy a good common to them all. But it bears an uncomfortable similarity to our fiscal predicament. It is rational for anyone benefiting from a government program to protect whatever benefits he receives, and try to gain more. It is similarly rational for a taxpayer to try to minimize his taxes or seek to cut them.

---

28. *http://www.sciencemag.org/content/162/3859/1243.full*

So all of these citizens acting rationally to increase their benefits and decrease their taxes create the tragedy of the fiscal commons. The result is a mountain of debt that threatens America's long-term fiscal health. Just as the pasture is eventually destroyed, so too is the American government's fiscal soundness.

How do we avoid the Tragedy of the Commons? By instituting some form of constraint on individual or group behavior. Some would argue that that can be a moral constraint, where individuals with a moral sense of responsibility for the whole control their more selfish impulses. But Hardin argued against the effectiveness of a moral constraint, because selfish individuals and groups will take advantage of those constrained by moral qualms.

Our experience with the federal budget argues against the moral constraint as well. "Protect what you have and try to get more" seems to be the guiding principle for budgetary politics, and don't worry about the size of the deficit, the enormity of the debt, and the burden we are dumping on our children and grandchildren.

The more effective constraint to avoid the tragedy of the commons comes from individuals collectively agreeing to limit grazing for the good of the whole. And that appears to be the only way to keep us from the tragedy of the fiscal commons. America needs a collective agreement that we must institute a global constraint on our budget to avoid destroying our fiscal future.

The Deficit in 21st Century Politics

The evidence is clear: running against the size of the deficit itself gains very little traction among American voters. That does not mean the deficit is irrelevant, particularly given its current size and future prospects. Deficits are like credit card debt. We rock along happily building up more and more credit card debt until one day the credit limit is reached, a purchase is declined, the payments come due, and then the credit card debt becomes a huge problem. But until a crisis is reached things look fine, or at least fine enough so that people vote on other issues.

In some ways conservatives face the same challenge making the deficit a voting issue that liberals have had making global warming or campaign finance reform voting issues.

All three are relatively abstract issues where voters see little clear and direct impact on their lives. Voters may admit that all three are problems, but they are primarily problems in the future, problems that may happen, and problems on which there is substantial disagreement about their seriousness and effects. All three are top-down issues where the threat is perceived and articulated by elites, PhDs, and editorial board writers, none of whom have been known to sway the opinions of large groups of voters.

Contrast those three issues with unemployment or illegal immigration, bottom-up issues where voters see and feel the direct impact of rising unemployment or illegal immigration in their communities on a daily basis, and where the impact is often felt more strongly on Main Street than on faculties or in editorial board rooms. Bottom-up issues have far more juice in politics, are more tied to emotions, and are therefore more motivating as voting issues than top-down issues.

And at least on the deficit, conservatives have a Chicken Little problem, where sky-is-falling scenarios have repeatedly failed to come true. How many years have economists told us that sky-high deficits create sky-high interest rates? Government's demand for borrowed money will crowd out private borrowers and drive interest rates through the roof, so the argument goes. Yet at the very time our deficits have grown to breathtaking proportions, interest rates have remained as close to zero as the Federal Reserve can keep them. The effect on interest rates has been precisely the opposite of what we were told to fear.

Messaging on Taxes, Spending, Deficits, and Debt

So how should Republicans talk about restoring fiscal sanity? Should they just ignore the problem because there is little political benefit in addressing it? How do they avoid becoming scolds who demand that voters take fiscal medicine they are not convinced they need to take? Can Republicans be popular and responsible at the same time?

There is ample evidence in public opinion research to suggest that voters are at least concerned about the level of federal spending and debt, even if it is not a top voting issue.

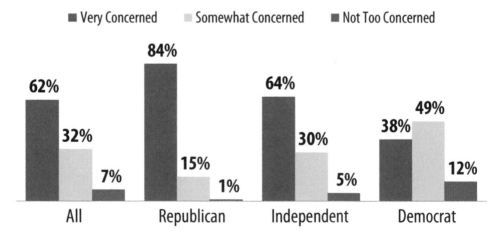

Concern About Federal Spending and Debt by Political Party

"How concerned are you about the federal government's current level of spending and debt—very concerned, somewhat concerned, or not too concerned?"

■ Very Concerned   ▪ Somewhat Concerned   ■ Not Too Concerned

Source: Resurgent Republic/North Star Opinion Research, National Survey of Likely Voters, April 25-27, 2010

Figure 4–4

When more than three-fifths of the country is "very concerned" about the federal government's spending and debt, there is a large audience that is willing to listen to ways to address the problem.

A majority of the country says that America's debt to China is a very serious problem. Two-thirds of Republicans, a majority of Independents, and a plurality of Democrats think our indebtedness to China is very serious.

Seriousness of America's Debt to China by Political Party

"China currently owns a larger share of America's debt than any other foreign country. How big a problem do you think that is for America: very serious, somewhat serious, or not too serious?"

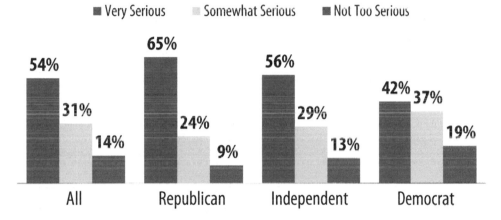

Source: Resurgent Republic/North Star Opinion Research, National Survey of Registered Voters, August 28-31, 2011

Figure 4-5

Even though the public may share a widespread concern about the size of the deficit, it splits sharply along partisan lines over ways to reduce it. Yet even on that question some common ground exists. First, voters believe the deficit is more of a spending than a revenue problem:

Reduce Deficit by Raising Taxes or Controlling Spending by Political Party

"Which statement comes closer to your view about reducing the federal deficit: **A)** We need more tax revenue as well as spending cuts to reduce the federal deficit. We will never get the deficit under control unless we make the difficult but necessary decision to raise taxes. **B)** Our federal deficit is a result of too much spending in Washington, not too little tax revenue. Instead of raising taxes on anyone, Congress should make the difficult but necessary decisions to get spending under control."

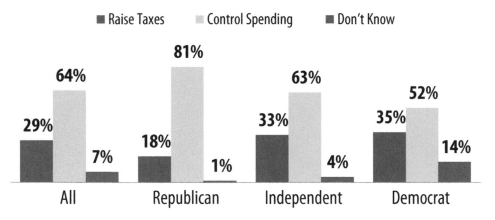

Source: Resurgent Republic/North Star Opinion Research, National Survey of Registered Voters, March 1-3, 2011

Figure 4-6

Voters overwhelmingly believe that the deficit is driven more by excessive spending than insufficient taxing. When even a majority of Democrats says the problem is spending more than it is revenue, it becomes clear that controlling spending is the higher priority for reducing the deficit.

Framed another way, voters do not believe we can tax our way out of the deficit. Even when the question limits higher taxes to "the wealthy," a majority of the country still says restraining spending is a higher priority than raising taxes.

Raise Taxes on Wealthy versus Restrain Spending and Reform Tax Code by Political Party

"[W]hich one [do] you agree with more: **Congressman A** says we need to raise taxes on the wealthy. We must have more tax revenue if we are ever going to reduce the deficit and make the wealthy pay their fair share. **Congressman B** says we will never tax our way out of the deficit. The way to reduce the deficit is to restrain government spending and reform our tax code to generate more economic growth."

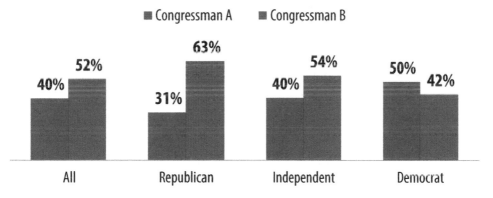

Source: Resurgent Republic/North Star Opinion Research, National Survey of Registered Voters, April 30-May 3, 2012

Figure 4-7

But voters also believe more revenue has got to be part of the solution, just a smaller part than spending cuts.

Preferred Mix of Spending Cuts and Tax Increases to Reduce the Deficit by Political Party

"Which of the following options do you prefer to reduce the federal deficit: a plan that proposes all spending cuts, more spending cuts than tax increases, an equal amount of spending cuts and tax increases, more tax increases than spending cuts, or all tax increases?"

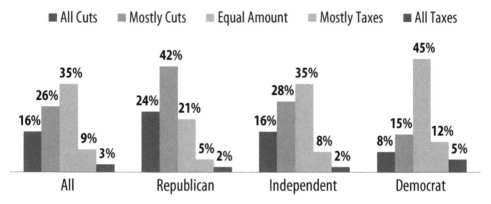

Source: Resurgent Republic/North Star Opinion Research, National Survey of Registered Voters, February 18-21, 2013

Figure 4-8

There are limits on the maximum federal tax rate that voters think is justified. Eight out of ten Americans think the maximum percentage the federal government should take from any individual should not be more than 30 percent. In contrast to many fiscal issues, remarkable bipartisan agreement exists on this question, with 87 percent of Republicans, 78 percent of Independents, and 74 percent of Democrats saying the maximum federal take should be no more than 30 percent.

Desired Maximum for All Federal Taxes

"What do you think is the maximum percentage that the federal government should take from any individual's income: ten percent, fifteen percent, twenty percent, thirty percent, forty percent, or fifty percent or more?"

	All	Republican	Independent	Democrat
10 Percent	27%	26%	24%	30%
15 Percent	16%	18%	16%	16%
20 Percent	22%	27%	22%	17%
30 Percent	14%	16%	16%	11%
40 Percent	4%	2%	4%	7%
50+ Percent	3%	1%	4%	4%

Source: Resurgent Republic / North Star Opinion Research,
National Survey of Registered Voters, August 28-31, 2011

Figure 4-9

Yet considering the maximum 2014 federal income tax rate of 39.6 percent, the Social Security tax of 6.2 percent, and the Medicare tax of 2.35 percent, the maximum federal take for high-income earners stands at 48.15 percent. And if that high-income earner is self-employed, the Social Security tax is 12.4 percent and the Medicare tax 3.8 percent, producing a total federal tax rate of 55.8 percent. Those are levels only 3 percent of Americans find acceptable.

How to Frame the Argument for Cutting Spending

Clearly some phrases are more powerful than others when making the case for cutting spending. The most powerful is "we have got to stop spending money we don't have."

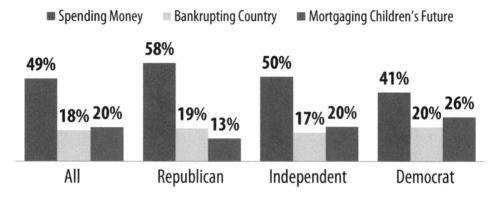

Best Wording on Cutting Spending by Political Party

"Which of the following do you think is the strongest and most powerful statement?
A) We have got to stop spending money we don't have; **B)** We have got to stop
bankrupting the country; **C)** We have got to stop mortgaging our children's future."

■ Spending Money   ■ Bankrupting Country   ■ Mortgaging Children's Future

Source: Resurgent Republic / North Star Opinion Research,
National Survey of Registered Voters, March 1-3, 2011

Figure 4-10

Indeed, the argument to stop spending money we don't have even trumps the argument to protect specific popular programs.

Stop Spending Money We Don't Have versus Slashing Spending on Programs by Political Party

"[W]hich one [do] you agree with more: **Congressman A** says we should not cut $100 billion out of current federal spending. Cutting that much means slashing funding for important programs like education, the Environmental Protection Agency, and border security. **Congressman B** says we should cut $100 billion out of current federal spending. Individuals and families are making do with less, and the government needs to do the same. We have got to stop spending money we don't have."

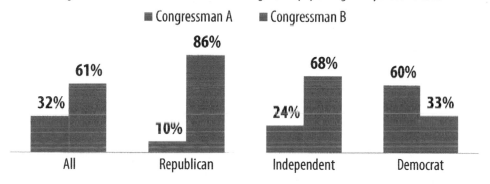

Source: Resurgent Republic / North Star Opinion Research,
National Survey of Registered Voters, March 1-3, 2011

Figure 4-11

Entitlement Programs

Framing a message on controlling entitlement programs is particularly challenging, because of the overwhelming popularity of programs like Social Security and Medicare. Making the case in fiscal terms, that we must reform entitlements because otherwise we will never balance the budget, is a losing argument.

Getting the Deficit Under Control versus Not Balancing the Budget on the Backs of Seniors and the Poor by Political Party

"[W]hich one [do] you agree with more: **Congressman A** says we should not balance the budget on the backs of our seniors and the poor. We need to cut back federal spending, but Social Security, Medicare, and Medicaid should be off limits; **Congressman B** says we will never get the deficit under control without making at least some adjustments in Social Security, Medicare, and Medicaid, because those three programs make up more than half of all federal domestic spending."

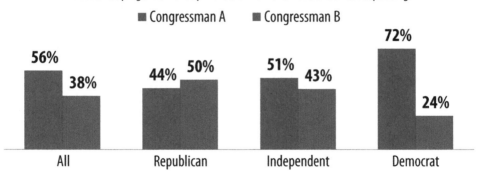

Source: Resurgent Republic/North Star Opinion Research, National Survey of Registered Voters, August 28-31, 2011

Figure 4-12

On the other hand, making the argument for reform because it is the only way to save popular programs is more persuasive.

Take Social Security off the Table versus Save Social Security by Political Party

"[W]hich one [do] you agree with more: **Congressman A** says Social Security will not face budget problems until 2037, so we need to focus our attention on our immediate budget problems and leave Social Security alone. Take Social Security off the table. **Congressman B** says Social Security is in real trouble because of so many retiring baby boomers. We can save Social Security with minor benefit adjustments for people age 55 and under, and we should do that now rather than wait until the program faces a crisis."

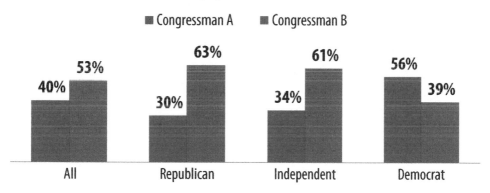

Source: Resurgent Republic/North Star Opinion Research,
National Survey of Registered Voters, August 28-31, 2011

Figure 4–13

Take Medicare off the Table versus Save Medicare by Political Party

"[W]hich one [do] you agree with more: **Congressman A** says we should not balance the budget on the backs of our seniors. We need to cut back federal spending, but Medicare should be off limits. Republican plans to privatize Medicare are a Trojan Horse that will end Medicare as we know it. **Congressman B** says the Medicare trustees have declared that Medicare will go broke if we do nothing because of all the retiring baby boomers. By giving people age 55 and under the choice of joining traditional Medicare or using Medicare dollars to buy a private health insurance plan, we can preserve and protect this important program for future generations."

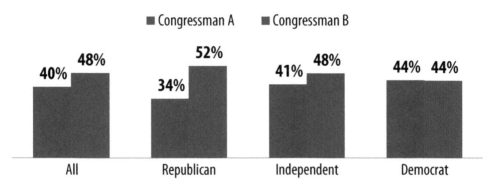

Source: Resurgent Republic/North Star Opinion Research,
National Survey of Registered Voters, April 30-May 3, 2012

Figure 4-14

But voters do believe that Social Security needs major reforms to preserve its long-term viability.

Social Security Needs Major or Minor Reforms by Political Party

"[W]hich one [do] you agree with more: **Congressman A** says that Social Security needs only minor reforms, with the primary goal being protecting benefits for seniors. Reforms like raising the retirement age or limiting benefits will break faith with workers who have paid into the system for decades. **Congressman B** says Social Security needs major reforms in order to maintain the long-term viability of the program and save the federal budget. We need to consider raising the retirement age for younger workers, as well as limiting benefits for wealthy retirees."

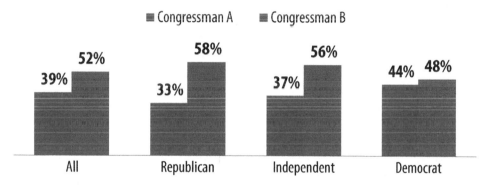

Source: Resurgent Republic/North Star Opinion Research,
National Survey of Registered Voters, January 12-16, 2011

Figure 4–15

A Balanced Budget Amendment

The most effective constraint on fiscal irresponsibility is a requirement for a balanced budget, already employed in one way or another by forty-nine states. Perhaps that is why large majorities of Americans have historically supported a balanced budget amendment to the U.S. Constitution that would extend that requirement to the federal government.

Yes, there are lots of reasons why the federal government's budget is different from those in state governments. But posing those arguments against the case for a balanced budget amendment fails to persuade a majority of Americans.

Balanced Budget Amendment is a Good or Bad Idea by Political Party

"[W]hich one [do] you agree with more: **Congressman A** says a balanced budget amendment to the U.S. Constitution is a bad idea. The federal budget is not like a family budget, and we need the flexibility to respond to economic needs and emergencies. **Congressman B** says a balanced budget amendment to the U.S. Constitution is a good idea. That is the only way we will restore fiscal responsibility, create jobs, and stop spending money we don't have."

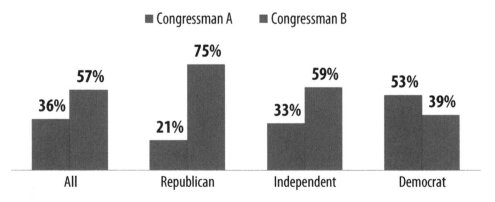

Source: Resurgent Republic/North Star Opinion Research,
National Survey of Registered Voters, August 28-31, 2011

Figure 4-16

Should or Should Not Adopt a Balanced Budget Amendment by Political Party

"[W]hich one [do] you agree with more: **Congressman A** says we should not adopt a constitutional amendment to balance the budget. That could force draconian cuts in Medicare and national defense, and hurt the government's ability to respond to emergencies like 9/11. **Congressman B** says we should adopt a constitutional amendment to balance the budget. With a $13 trillion national debt that is undermining our economy, it is the only way we will instill some fiscal discipline in politicians and stop them from bankrupting the country."

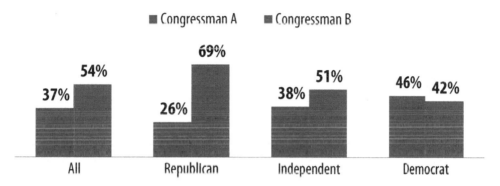

Source: *Resurgent Republic/North Star Opinion Research, National Survey of Likely Voters, June 20-23, 2010*

Figure 4–17

Of course our fiscal hole is so deep that a balanced budget seems like a mirage, even though we are only fifteen years removed from the last balanced federal budget. Perhaps intermediate steps will be required. Ultimately a global constraint around incentives that push in the opposite direction is the only way to impose fiscal sanity.

Some Republicans fear a requirement for a balanced budget will lead to massive tax increases. There is little doubt that producing a balanced budget will require more revenue as well as spending cuts. But we will never tax our way to a balanced budget. Confiscating every penny of income made by the top one percent of earners would keep the federal government going for a grand total of sixty days. So producing a balanced federal budget will inevitably require more spending cuts than tax increases.

Passing a balanced budget amendment requires presidential leadership. It takes a president to persuade the country that out-of-control deficits damage the top priorities of economic growth and job creation. It takes a president to convince Americans that everyone needs to contribute something to protect the well-being of the country and the prosperity of future generations.

And it takes a president who views himself as the president of all the people, not just those who voted for him. It demands someone to call us to rise above our own selfish interests and do something for the good of all. It demands an inspirational figure to call us to a common purpose and support a global constraint on our individual interests for the good of the nation and the economy.

Dos and Don'ts

Public opinion research clearly indicates that some fiscal messages are far more effective than others:

- **Do** make the case that the only way to cure the deficit problem is by growing the private sector economy. We will never "tax our way out of the deficit." Only by growing the private sector economy will we generate the additional revenue necessary to close the yawning budget deficit.

- **Do** make the case for spending restraint by arguing that reform is the only way to save critically important programs. The impending retirement of the baby boom generation creates enormous pressure on entitlement programs like Social Security and Medicare. Making reasonable adjustments in those programs—both to the benefit structure and the funding mechanisms—are critical to ensure their survival. We need to "preserve and protect" programs on which millions of seniors depend.

- **Do** talk about budget numbers in personal terms. The best way to make enormous budget numbers meaningful is to do so in terms of "per person" or "per family."

- **Do** argue for adopting a balanced budget amendment to the U.S. Constitution. Popular support for such an amendment has been strong over the years, and it is the best way to create a global constraint around a process where all the incentives push for greater spending and lower taxes.

- **Do** talk about fiscal responsibility as a means to economic growth, not as the end in itself. Voters always place a higher priority on problems they see and feel on a daily basis than they do on abstract problems they may feel sometime in the future. That means that jobs and economic growth will always be a higher priority than whether or not the government's books are balanced. The top priority should always be on a growth agenda that promotes economic expansion and creates private sector jobs.

On the other hand, some messages just do not work:

- **Do not** argue for controlling entitlement spending because "we have to get spending under control to cut the deficit and balance the budget." Voters place a far higher priority on protecting beneficiaries than they do on whether the government's books are balanced.

- **Do not** talk about budget numbers just in the aggregate because the numbers are so abstract they are meaningless. "The federal debt has increased under President Obama from ten trillion to seventeen trillion dollars." So what? Voters have a hard time understanding what that means for them and their lives.

Conclusion

Resolving our fiscal dilemma will take years of work, strong presidential leadership, and sustained economic growth. Republicans need to lead that effort. It cannot be framed in terms of what is best for the federal budget or for the deficit, because most voters do not necessarily connect fiscal responsibility to better outcomes for their own lives or those of their children. It should be framed in the context of what is best for our economy, what is best for the beneficiaries of government programs, and what is best for future generations.

ABORTION

For forty years abortion has been one of the most emotional and value-laden debates in American life. The 1973 Supreme Court decision in *Roe v. Wade* ensured that the debate over abortion would be never-ending by trying to impose a national solution on a country torn with disagreement. Wise justices would have allowed the issue to play out through our democratic institutions first, with different laws following the different value systems of the various states. But wisdom did not prevail that day. As a result we have ongoing, contentious, seemingly endless debate about when and under what circumstances abortion should be allowed.

Some of those hoping to resurrect Republican political fortunes at the presidential level have advised Republicans to abandon their historical pro-life position. They argue that to become nationally competitive in the 21st century, the party must become pro-choice.

Based on current public opinion research, that advice is wrong. The Republican Party can and should maintain a mainstream pro-life position on abortion.

The key word is "mainstream." Too many Republican candidates in recent years have thrown away winnable races by promoting a pro-life position so extreme that it immediately defines the candidate as outside mainstream political thinking.

So what does a mainstream pro-life position look like? What do voters think about abortion today?

Current Public Opinion on Abortion

On the broad outlines of abortion policy, public opinion has changed remarkably little in the forty years since *Roe v. Wade* made abortion legal throughout the country. Gallup has asked the following question over those four decades: "Do you think abortions should be legal under any circumstances, legal only under certain circumstances, or illegal in all circumstances?"

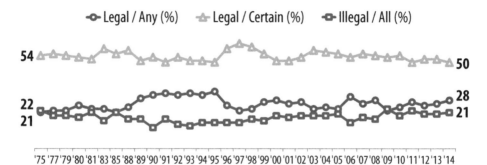

Circumstances Under Which Abortion Should be Legal: 1975-2014

"Do you think abortions should be legal under any circumstances, legal only under certain circumstances, or illegal in all circumstances?"

Source: Gallup data from surveys taken 1975-2014. Copyright 2015 Gallup, Inc. all rights reserved

Figure 5-1

In 1975, 22 percent of Americans thought abortion should be illegal in all circumstances; today that figure is 21 percent. In 1975, 21 percent thought abortion should be legal in all circumstances; today it is 28 percent. In 1975, the majority of Americans—54 percent—thought abortion should be legal in some circumstances but not others; today that figure is 50 percent. For the subject of major debate over four decades, opinions on abortion are remarkably stable.

Since most Americans believe abortion should be allowed in at least some circumstances, a majority has consistently opposed overturning the *Roe v. Wade* decision.

Should the Supreme Court Overturn Roe v. Wade: 1989-2012

"The 1973 *Roe v. Wade* decision established a woman's constitutional right to an abortion, at least in the first three months of pregnancy. Would you like to see the Supreme Court completely overturn its *Roe v. Wade* decision or not?"

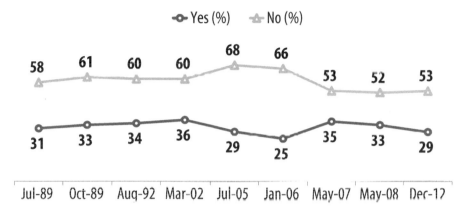

Source: Gallup data from surveys taken 1989-2012. Copyright 2015 Gallup, Inc. all rights reserved

Figure 5-2

Consequently it is not surprising that, by 61 to 37 percent, a large majority opposes a constitutional amendment "to ban abortion in all circumstances, except in cases necessary to save the life of the mother."[29]

Circumstances for Abortion

Because the overwhelming majority of Americans believes abortion should be allowed in some circumstances but not others, the debate revolves around the circumstances under which it should be allowed. At least at either end of the spectrum, the country has reached a clear consensus. Three-fourths of Americans reject the argument that abortion should never be allowed under any circumstances, and three-fourths reject allowing abortion in every imaginable circumstance.

---

29. *http://www.gallup.com/poll/20203/Americans-Favor-Parental-Involvement-Teen-Abortion-Decisions.aspx#2*

Prohibiting abortion in all circumstances, or allowing it in all circumstances, offers a certain intellectual, logical, and moral consistency. But intellectual, logical, and moral consistency does not necessarily make a great political argument on an issue as complex as abortion. There may be a place for prophets who speak uncomfortable and unpopular truths to an oblivious world, but that place is not in elective office. Mainstream political candidates do not take positions on prominent issues that are opposed by three-fourths of Americans.

So where do Americans come down on abortion today? They are torn, and have been since *Roe v. Wade*. They truly wrestle with the morality of abortion and the circumstances under which it should be allowed. The issue is not an abstract discussion, but in fact is very personal: 61 percent of Americans know someone who has had an abortion.[30] So the chances are good that any aspiring political leader talking about abortion is talking to a woman who has had one, or about her mother or her daughter.

When asked if they are pro-life or pro-choice, Americans have split almost evenly over the past decade in Gallup data, with a July 2011 survey showing an exactly even split at 47 percent for each option.[31] But focus groups demonstrate that the labels "pro-choice" and "pro-life" disguise great variation in peoples' attitudes. Many "pro-choice" Americans want to prohibit abortions in some circumstances, while many "pro-life" people would allow abortion in some circumstances.

In the abstract, Americans value the concept of "choice"—51 percent say that the choice on abortion should be left up to the woman and her doctor.[32]

---

30. *http://publicreligion.org/site/wp-content/uploads/2011/06/Millenials-Abortion-and-Religion-Survey-Report.pdf*, p. 35

31. *http://www.gallup.com/poll/148880/Plenty-Common-Ground-Found-Abortion-Debate.aspx*, July 15-17 survey

32. *http://online.wsj.com/public/resources/documents/wsjnbc-10272009.pdf*, question 42

But they also recognize that the "choice" of an abortion is not like choosing a facelift or a new car. Sixty-five percent think abortion ends a human life, while only 26 percent think it does not.[33] Two-thirds of Americans say it would be a good thing to reduce the number of abortions performed in the United States, while only a quarter disagree.[34]

The 26 percent who think abortion does not end a human life, and the 26 percent who think it would *not* be a good thing to reduce the number of abortions, are virtually identical to the 25 percent who say abortion should be legal under any circumstances. Essentially one-fourth of Americans have no qualms about abortion. The other three-fourths have serious reservations.

33. *http://www.aei.org/wp-content/uploads/2014/01/-attitudes-about-abortion-an-aei-public-opinion-study_165237903059.pdf*, p. 4. This periodically updated review by Karlyn Bowman of the American Enterprise Institute is an excellent review of the broad array of questions asked about abortion over the years.

34. Ibid, p. 20

Americans overwhelmingly believe abortion should be legal when the woman's life is endangered, when the woman's physical health is endangered, or when pregnancy results from rape or incest. Six out of ten people who consider themselves "pro-life" support legal abortion in these circumstances.

Circumstances Under Which a Majority Believes Abortion Should be Legal

"Now I am going to read some specific situations under which an abortion might be considered. For each one, please say whether you think abortion should be legal in that situation, or illegal. How about when ..."

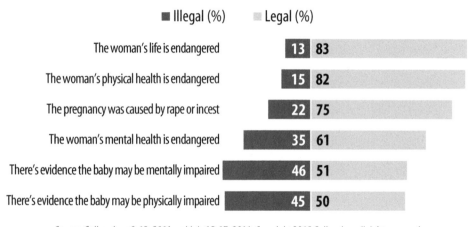

Figure 5-3

On the other hand, a majority does not believe abortion should be allowed just because the woman cannot afford to raise the child, does not want any more children, or is unmarried.

Circumstances Under Which a Majority Believes Abortion Should be Illegal

"Do you think it should be possible for a pregnant woman to obtain a legal abortion if:"

■ No (%)　　■ Yes (%)

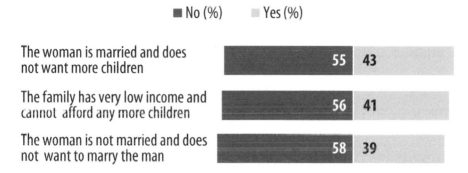

	No (%)	Yes (%)
The woman is married and does not want more children	55	43
The family has very low income and cannot afford any more children	56	41
The woman is not married and does not want to marry the man	58	39

Source: National Opinion Research Center, 2008.

Figure 5-4

Restrictions on Abortion

Americans hold dramatically different views on abortion depending on the stage of pregnancy. By a two-to-one margin, they believe abortion in the first trimester should be legal. But by more than two-to-one they think abortion in the second trimester should be illegal. The margin of those who believe abortion should be illegal in the third trimester surpasses five-to-one.

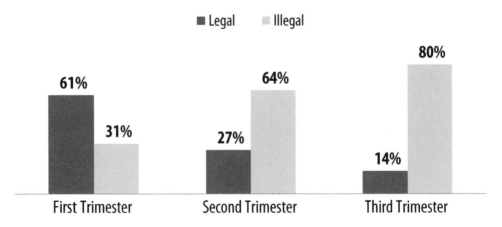

Abortion Legal or Illegal by Trimester

"Thinking more generally, do you think abortion should generally be legal or generally illegal during each of the following stages of pregnancy?"

■ Legal   ▦ Illegal

First Trimester — 61% 31%
Second Trimester — 27% 64%
Third Trimester — 14% 80%

Source: Gallup, December 27-30, 2012. Copyright 2015 Gallup, Inc. all rights reserved

Figure 5-5

By huge margins, Americans support informed consent before having an abortion, parental consent before a minor can have an abortion, 24-hour waiting periods before having an abortion, and spousal notification. They also oppose partial birth abortion by more than a two-to-one margin.

Restrictions on Abortion

"Do you favor or oppose each of the following proposals?"

■ Oppose (%)   ▨ Favor (%)

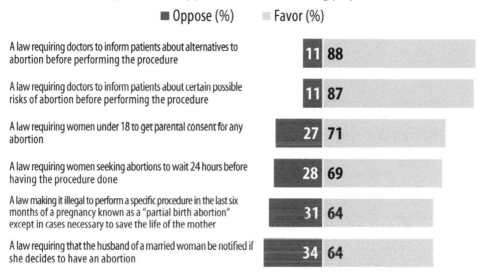

A law requiring doctors to inform patients about alternatives to abortion before performing the procedure — 11 | 88

A law requiring doctors to inform patients about certain possible risks of abortion before performing the procedure — 11 | 87

A law requiring women under 18 to get parental consent for any abortion — 27 | 71

A law requiring women seeking abortions to wait 24 hours before having the procedure done — 28 | 69

A law making it illegal to perform a specific procedure in the last six months of a pregnancy known as a "partial birth abortion" except in cases necessary to save the life of the mother — 31 | 64

A law requiring that the husband of a married woman be notified if she decides to have an abortion — 34 | 64

Source: Gallup, July 15-17, 2011. Copyright 2015 Gallup, Inc. all rights reserved

Figure 5-6

Federal Funding for Abortion

Americans have also reached a consensus on using federal tax dollars to pay for abortions: they oppose it. Opposition is consistent over time, and with different question wording. For example, Republicans, Independents, and Democrats all opposed using public funds in ObamaCare to pay for abortions.

Attitudes about Public Funding of Abortion by Political Party

"Do you support or oppose allowing abortions to be paid for by public funds under a health care reform bill?"

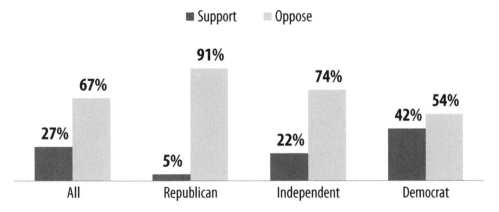

Source: Quinnipiac, January 2010

Figure 5-7

Differences by Gender

Much discussion about abortion revolves around a political candidate's appeal to women, especially women of childbearing age for whom abortion is a particularly personal issue. While somewhat more women than men favor allowing abortion in most circumstances, the most striking aspect about abortion attitudes by gender is the *similarity* between men and women, not the differences.

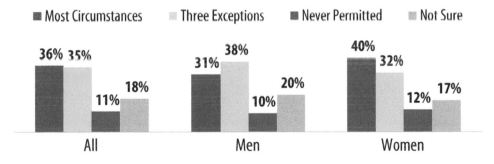

Circumstances for Abortion by Gender

"Which of the following views about abortion comes closest to your own: **A)** Abortion should be allowed in most circumstances; **B)** Abortion should only be permitted in cases of rape, incest, or danger to the woman's life; **C)** Abortion should never be permitted; **D)** Are you not sure about this?"

■ Most Circumstances   ▨ Three Exceptions   ■ Never Permitted   ▨ Not Sure

Source: Bipartisan Policy Center / North Star Opinion Research, National Survey of Registered Voters, February 18-21, 2013

Figure 5-8

On conditions that must be met before having an abortion, differences between men and women are negligible. Women are actually slightly more supportive than men on requiring a 24-hour waiting period before receiving an abortion, requiring parental consent before a minor can have an abortion, and requiring doctors to inform patients about the risks of the procedure.

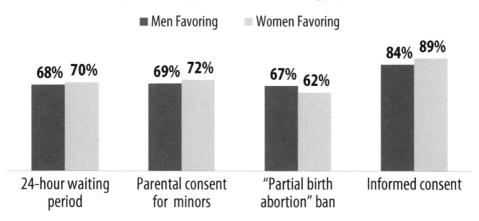

Restrictions on Abortion by Gender

"Do you favor or oppose each of the following proposals?"

■ Men Favoring   ▨ Women Favoring

Source: Gallup, July 15-17, 2011. Copyright 2015 Gallup, Inc. all rights reserved

Figure 5-9

Differences by Age

Public opinion data does not support the argument that young people are strongly pro-choice on abortion. Indeed, voters under 30 years old have almost identical views to those age 30 to 49 years old. Only 39 percent of young voters think abortion should be permitted in most circumstances, while 50 percent think it should be permitted only in the cases of rape, incest, the life of the mother, or never permitted at all. Comparable figures for 30- to 49-year-olds are 38 percent most circumstances and 44 percent three exceptions or not at all.

Seniors are least likely to favor abortion in most circumstances—27 percent—but the percentage of seniors favoring abortion in the three circumstances or not at all is 52 percent, almost identical to the 50 percent among young people.

In other words, age—like gender—is a poor predictor of views on abortion.

Circumstances for Abortion by Age

"Which of the following views about abortion comes closest to your own: **A)** Abortion should be allowed in most circumstances; **B)** Abortion should only be permitted in cases of rape, incest, or danger to the woman's life; **C)** Abortion should never be permitted; **D)** Are you not sure about this?"

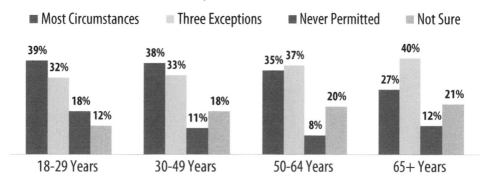

Source: Bipartisan Policy Center / North Star Opinion Research, National Survey of Registered Voters, February 18-21, 2013

Figure 5-10

Differences by Church Attendance

Unlike the relatively modest differences on abortion by gender and age, differences by frequency of church attendance are stark and consistent. That should be unsurprising on an issue with such a strong moral component as abortion. The more religiously active the voter, the more likely he or she will be to want to restrict abortions. Indeed, among voters who attend church at least once a week, the proportion who favors abortion in most circumstances is only 22 percent—almost equivalent to the proportion who believes abortion should never be permitted at 20 percent.

On the other hand, among voters who never attend church, the overwhelming preference is for allowing abortion in most circumstances—54 percent. A miniscule 2 percent of non-religious voters believe abortion should never be permitted.

These differences in views on abortion by church attendance are consistent by gender, age, race, and region. Regardless of other demographic characteristics, church attendance is one of the best predictors of views on abortion.

Circumstances for Abortion by Church Attendance

"Which of the following views about abortion comes closest to your own: **A)** Abortion should be allowed in most circumstances; **B)** Abortion should only be permitted in cases of rape, incest, or danger to the woman's life; **C)** Abortion should never be permitted; **D)** Are you not sure about this?"

■ Most Circumstances   Three Exceptions   ■ Never Permitted   Not Sure

At Least Once/Wk: 22% 41% 20% 18%
Few Times Mo/Yr: 40% 34% 8% 19%
Never Attend: 54% 27% 2% 17%

Source: Bipartisan Policy Center / North Star Opinion Research, National Survey of Registered Voters, February 18-21, 2013

Figure 5-11

Dos and Don'ts

The data clearly shows that Republicans can be nationally competitive in the 21st century as a mainstream pro-life party. So what does a mainstream pro-life position look like? Following are some guidelines:

- **Do** recognize the moral ambivalence with which the vast majority of Americans approach the abortion issue.

- **Do** demonstrate compassion for women wrestling with an unwanted pregnancy.

- **Do** remember that any audience with female members likely contains some women who have had abortions.

- **Do** project a tone of tolerance to those with different views.

- **Do** be exceedingly sensitive if you find yourself compelled to discuss medical aspects of abortion, especially if you are male.

- **Do** support legal abortion in the cases of rape, incest, or the life of the mother.

- **Do** support common sense restrictions on abortion including informed consent before having an abortion, parental consent before a minor can have an abortion, and a 24-hour waiting period before having an abortion.

- **Do** oppose late-term abortions.

- **Do** make Democrats defend their extreme positions, especially late-term abortions.

On the other hand, here are some don'ts for a mainstream pro-life position:

- **Do not** come across as condemning and harshly judgmental toward those who have had an abortion or those with whom you disagree.

- **Do not** argue that a woman who has been raped should be denied access to an abortion.

- **Do not** place abortion at the top of your political agenda. Doing so splits the Republican coalition between religious conservatives and libertarians. You need both to win.

- **Do not** call abortion "murder." When three out of five Americans know someone who has had an abortion, labeling those women as "murderers" will never persuade people to join your side.

- **Do not** make being pro-life a litmus test for being a good Republican.

- **Do not** try to restrict the activities of infertility centers that are trying to help couples have a child. (You are supposed to be *pro*-life, after all.)

Talking about abortion in American politics is like handling nitroglycerin—it should be done with extreme care. If your audience contains women, chances are very good that you are talking to someone who is extraordinarily sensitive about the topic. If you say the wrong thing, you can blow up your candidacy in an instant. Get your position down pat, know why you think what you do, repeat it endlessly, and move on to other issues with greater potential to win adherents to your side and less risk for destroying your campaign.

★ ★ ★ **6** ★ ★ ★

GAY RIGHTS

The American electorate has changed so dramatically on a few issues that positions supported by a majority of voters only a few years ago now seem like relics of the past. There is simply no way that Republicans can seem like a modern political party with widespread appeal in the New America unless they adjust to the new reality on at least a few of their long-standing policy positions. Just as the Democrats had to change their stance on the death penalty and welfare reform to become nationally competitive again after 1988, public opinion data points to areas where Republicans need to adapt to a new world. Foremost in this area are gay rights.

On no issue in American life have views changed as rapidly as they have on gay rights. At a time when views on other moral issues—like abortion—have remained remarkably stable, a revolution has occurred in less than one generation on gay rights. It is hard to appreciate the extent and pace of change on this issue. Check out the change in only the last decade on whether gay and lesbian relations are "morally acceptable" or "morally wrong."

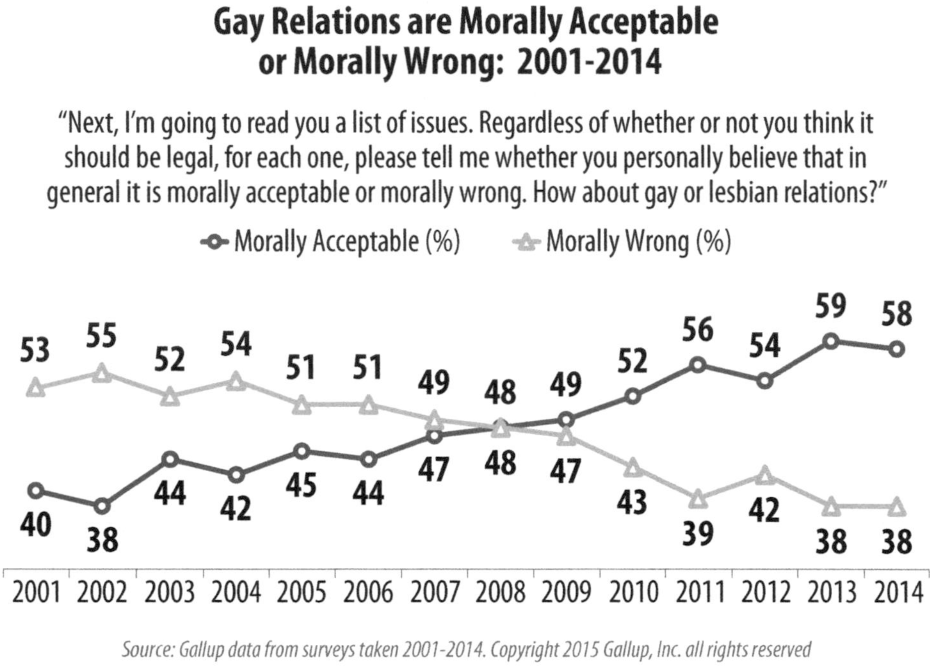

Gay Relations are Morally Acceptable
or Morally Wrong: 2001-2014

"Next, I'm going to read you a list of issues. Regardless of whether or not you think it should be legal, for each one, please tell me whether you personally believe that in general it is morally acceptable or morally wrong. How about gay or lesbian relations?"

—◆— Morally Acceptable (%)   —▲— Morally Wrong (%)

53	55	52	54	51	51	49	48	49	52	56	54	59	58
40	38	44	42	45	44	47	48	47	43	39	42	38	38
2001	2002	2003	2004	2005	2006	2007	2008	2009	2010	2011	2012	2013	2014

Source: Gallup data from surveys taken 2001-2014. Copyright 2015 Gallup, Inc. all rights reserved

Figure 6-1

America has moved from a country where, from 2001-2004, a steady majority believed gay and lesbian relations were morally wrong to a steady majority who, by 2011-2014, consider those relations morally acceptable. The lines crossed in 2008 at the end of the last Bush administration.

Gay Marriage

Approval of gay marriage has lagged behind the proportion of Americans who think gay and lesbian relations are morally acceptable, but only by four years. As of 2013, a majority of Americans supports gay marriage.

Gay Marriage Should or Should Not be Legal: 1996-2014

"Do you think marriages between same-sex couples should or should not be recognized by the law as valid, with the same rights as traditional marriages?"

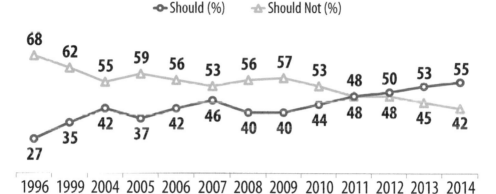

Source: Gallup data from surveys taken 1996-2014. Copyright 2015 Gallup, Inc. all rights reserved

Figure 6-2

There are surprisingly few issues where the age of the respondent is one of the strongest predictors of political views. One exception is gay rights. Young Americans inhabit a different world than their elders when it comes to tolerance and acceptance of gay relationships. On gay marriage, the breakpoint is at age 50, with majorities younger than 50 supporting gay marriage and majorities over 50 opposed.

Gay Marriage Should or Should Not be Legal by Age

"Do you think marriages between same-sex couples should or should not be recognized by the law as valid, with the same rights as traditional marriages?"

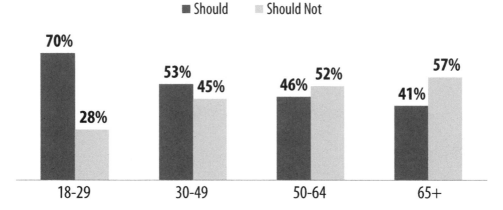

Source: Gallup, May 2-7, 2013. Copyright 2015 Gallup, Inc. all rights reserved

Figure 6-3

Sharp differences occur by party, with a strong majority of Democrats in favor of gay marriage and a strong majority of Republicans opposed. But look at the Independents who hold the balance of power in an evenly divided country. Independents look far more like Democrats than Republicans on this issue. By an 18-point margin, Independents now say they support gay marriage.

Gay Marriage Should or Should Not be Legal by Political Party

"Do you think marriages between same-sex couples should or should not be recognized by the law as valid, with the same rights as traditional marriages?"

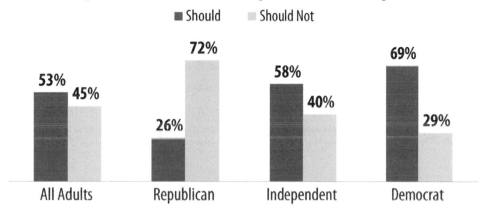

Source: Gallup, May 2-7, 2013. Copyright 2015 Gallup, Inc. all rights reserved

Figure 6–4

Despite the overwhelming opposition to gay marriage by Republicans overall, the striking generation gap persists regardless of party affiliation. As of March, 2014, 61 percent of Republicans under age 30 support gay marriage, while just 35 percent oppose it.[35]

---

35. *http://www.pewresearch.org/fact-tank/2014/03/10/61-of-young-republicans-favor-same-sex-marriage/*

Changing Minds on Gay Marriage

Almost all Americans who have changed their minds about gay marriage have gone from opposition to support. Virtually all people who continue to oppose gay marriage have held that view consistently. Only 2 percent of those who have changed their position have gone from support to opposition, but more than one-fourth—28 percent—of gay marriage supporters say they changed their minds from opposition to support. The most common reasons given for their change of heart are knowing someone who is homosexual, becoming more open about the issue, and giving it more thought as they have grown older.[36]

36. *http://www.people-press.org/2013/03/20/growing-support-for-gay-marriage-changed-minds-and-changing-demographics/*

Reasons for Changing Minds on Gay Marriage

"What made you change your mind about same-sex marriage?"

% Among Supporters Who Have Changed Their Minds

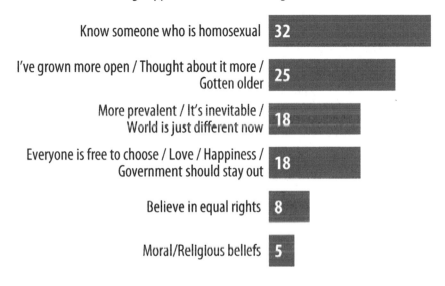

Know someone who is homosexual	32
I've grown more open / Thought about it more / Gotten older	25
More prevalent / It's inevitable / World is just different now	18
Everyone is free to choose / Love / Happiness / Government should stay out	18
Believe in equal rights	8
Moral/Religious beliefs	5

Source: Pew Research Center, March 13-17, 2013

Figure 6-5

What People Said

"My best friend from high school is a gay man and he deserves the same rights; they are in a committed relationship."

"Old fashioned ignorance, I grew up a little bit."

"Just the change in society, it's time."

"More people are happier if that's how they want to live."

"There is one judge and I am not that one judge."

Gay Parenting

Americans now think that same-sex couples can be as good parents as heterosexual couples by a two-to-one margin: 64 to 32 percent as of 2013, up 10 percentage points from ten years earlier. Interestingly, no significant difference arises between adults who are parents themselves and those who are not.

Once again the age differences are striking. Only a bare majority of seniors thinks same-sex couples can be equally good parents, 53 to 41 percent. But among adults age 32 and younger, support for gay parenting is overwhelming at 78 to 18 percent.

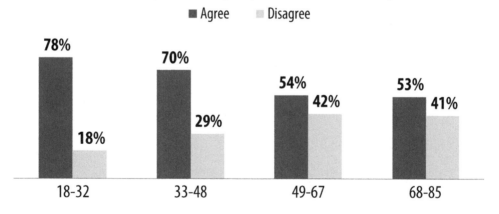

Gay Parenting by Age

"Same-sex couples can be as good parents as heterosexual couples..."

■ Agree   Disagree

78%	70%	54% 42%	53% 41%
18%	29%		
18-32	33-48	49-67	68-85

Source: Pew Research Center, March 13-17, 2013

Figure 6-6

Gay Marriage and Interracial Marriage

Public opinion on gay marriage bears striking similarities to public opinion on interracial marriage. We have more years of data on interracial marriage than gay marriage, so the starting and ending points show more divergence, but the pattern of enormous opinion change on this emotional and value-laden issue is similar.

In 1958, only 4 percent of Americans approved of "marriage between blacks and whites," while 94 percent disapproved. By 1972, the approve-disapprove numbers on interracial marriage were 29 to 60 percent, similar to the 1996 numbers on gay marriage. The lines on interracial marriage crossed during the 1980s, so that by 1991 a plurality of Americans approved of interracial marriage—48 to 42 percent. By 2013, the 1958 numbers were almost completely reversed with 87 percent approving of marriage between blacks and whites and only 11 percent disapproving.

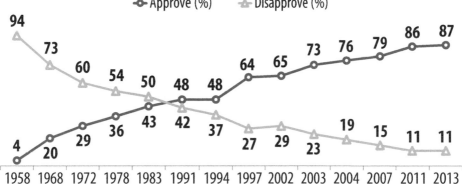

Approval of Interracial Marriage: 1958-2013

"Do you approve or disapprove of marriage between blacks and whites?"

Approve (%)   Disapprove (%)

Figure 6–7

The chart reflects a sea change in cultural norms about interracial marriage, stunning in its complete reversal of attitudes. In the 1950s marriage between blacks and whites was not only taboo, but against the law in many states including all fifteen in the southeast. Three unsuccessful attempts were made to pass a constitutional amendment banning interracial marriage throughout the country.[37]

The rationale for opposing interracial marriage in the past bears similarities to reasons offered today for opposing gay marriage. Many reasons were rooted in interpretations of scripture and judgments about God's will. A brief history lesson makes the point well.

In June of 1958 an interracial couple in Virginia, Richard Loving, who was white, and Mildred Jeter, who was black, went to Washington, D.C. to get married. They returned to their home in Virginia, one of the states that prohibited interracial marriage. They were arrested and pled guilty in state court, and were sentenced to a year in jail, suspended on the condition they leave the state and not return for twenty-five years. In his opinion Judge Leon Bazile reflected the views of the overwhelming majority of Americans at that time when he wrote:

> *Almighty God created the races white, black, yellow, malay and red, and he placed them on separate continents. And but for the interference with His arrangement there would be no cause for such marriages. The fact that He separated the races shows that He did not intend for the races to mix.*[38]

Nine years later, in *Loving v. Virginia*, the U.S. Supreme Court declared Virginia's Racial Integrity Act of 1924 unconstitutional. The Court held that that ban violated the equal protection clause of the 14th Amendment. But it would take more than twenty years for public opinion to change in support of that position. Based on the evidence today, public opinion on gay marriage is moving much faster.

---

37. *http://civilliberty.about.com/od/raceequalopportunity/tp/Interracial-Marriage-Laws-History-Timeline.htm*

38. *http://www.law.cornell.edu/supct/html/historics/USSC_CR_0388_0001_ZO.html*

Given the current attitudes of young people on gay marriage, one day, in the not-so-distant future, bans on gay marriage will seem as anachronistic as bans on interracial marriage do today.

Gay Rights and Abortion

While gay rights and abortion are frequently joined as cultural or moral issues, public opinion now makes a sharp distinction between the two. Americans have been, and likely will remain, torn about the morality of abortion. They are clearly uncomfortable with the moral implications, yet believe abortion should be legally available in at least some cases. That is one reason why public opinion on abortion has changed so little in broad outline in the last four decades. That is also why Republicans should remain the mainstream pro-life party.

Most Americans now believe gay and lesbian relationships are morally acceptable, and their number will increase dramatically over the next few decades. Elderly Americans who are opposed to gay relationships will die off and be replaced by young people who do not object to gay and lesbian relationships or same-sex marriages.

The progress of science is likely to lead in different directions on abortion and gay rights as well. The more we learn about neonatal development, the more difficult it will be to pretend that a fetus is not a human life. Science will likely strengthen the pro-life side of the abortion argument.

On the other hand, the more we learn about the origins of homosexuality, the more difficult it will be to believe that homosexuality is a choice. Science will likely strengthen the nature versus nurture side of the homosexuality debate. If rock-ribbed conservatives like Dick and Lynne Cheney can produce a gay daughter, the cause is probably not environmental. And if most gay people are born gay, rather than choose to be gay, that dramatically changes the gay rights debate.

The handwriting is on the wall about future acceptance of gay men and women in American life. When exalted conservative institutions like the United States military and the Boy Scouts of America openly accept gays, as they now do, the public debate is effectively over.

Dos and Don'ts

While the Republican Party does not need to support gay marriage to be competitive among young people, it does need to stop virulently opposing it. The 2008 Republican platform called for "a constitutional amendment that fully protects marriage as a union of a man and a woman, so that judges cannot make other arrangements equivalent to it."[39] In other words, it sought to adopt a constitutional amendment to ban gay marriage throughout the country.

The 2012 Republican platform eliminated the explicit call for a constitutional amendment to ban gay marriage, but did say "we believe that marriage, the union of one man and one woman must be upheld as the national standard, a goal to stand for, encourage, and promote through laws governing marriage."[40]

As of the end of 2014, gay marriage is legal in thirty-six states. How should Republicans react? Following are some dos and don'ts.

- **Do** reiterate the importance of healthy families as the foundation of civil society.

- **Do** talk about family as one of the core values of American life. For example: "Our country should value family, life, and hard work."

- **Do** oppose the imposition of gay marriage by judicial fiat in states opposed to it.

---

39. *http://www.gop.com/wp-content/uploads/2012/06/2008platform.pdf*, p. 53

40. *http://www.gop.com/wp-content/uploads/2012/08/2012GOPPlatform.pdf*, p. 31

- **Do** call for a state-by-state answer to gay marriage, where states with dramatically different values can adhere to their own value system. Part of the genius of our federal system is the opportunity for diverse sets of values to govern different states. States have traditionally handled marriage issues, and they deserve the right to continue to do so. Trying to impose one national answer on such an emotional and value-laden question as gay marriage will make it more difficult for the country to resolve this issue harmoniously.

On the other hand, here are some don'ts:

- **Do not** condemn non-traditional families. Doing so alienates the millions of American families that do not follow the traditional model of a married father and mother with children.

- **Do not** try to overturn gay marriage laws through federal intervention in states that have adopted them through democratic means like referenda or legislative votes. Doing so violates the Republican Party's principles of a limited federal government, individual liberty, and resolution of disputes through democratic means.

- **Do not** oppose any legal recognition of homosexual relationships. Opposing even civil unions for same-sex couples makes Republicans appear to be relics of the past.

- **Do not** oppose allowing homosexual couples to adopt children. Republicans rightly extol the virtues of strong and stable family units for raising children. Republicans look hypocritical opposing the right of stable same-sex couples to raise their own children and create strong family units.

Changing the Republican Party's stance on an issue as emotional and value-laden as gay rights will be extraordinarily difficult for many Republicans. Given their entrenched and deeply held beliefs, many rooted in Biblical passages, changing views on gay issues will border on sacrilege. It helps to remember, however, that for an earlier generation of Americans, changing its position on interracial marriage was equally gut-wrenching.

Public opinion has rendered its verdict on the morality of gay and lesbian relationships. That opinion will not be reversed. The only question is whether the Republican Party will acknowledge and adapt to this new reality.

★ ★ ★ 7 ★ ★ ★

HISPANIC VOTERS *and* IMMIGRATION REFORM

Hispanics have consistently voted for Democratic candidates for president since exit polls began, as have many new immigrants to America over the years. But the margin by which Hispanics prefer Democratic candidates matters, and will matter even more as Hispanics grow in number and become more critical in swing states like Florida, Colorado, Nevada, and New Mexico.

Unlike African-Americans, Hispanics are not yet locked into the Democratic Party. There is still time for Republicans to win substantial Hispanic support with the right candidate and the right message. But time is running out, and the political consequences are enormous. Republicans received vivid case studies about how to, and how not to, appeal to the Hispanic community in the period from 2004 to 2014.

George W. Bush demonstrated the potential for a Republican presidential candidate to win substantial support in the Hispanic community when he took 44 percent of the Hispanic vote nationally, and a majority of the Hispanic vote in the Sunbelt states in 2004. He did so by being sympathetic to Hispanic concerns, speaking a version of Spanish, advertising on Spanish-language TV and radio, and reaching out aggressively in the Hispanic community to seek Hispanic support. He also proposed comprehensive immigration reform that would have provided a path to citizenship for the eleven million undocumented immigrants in America.

Unfortunately 2004 is the high water mark for Hispanic support for a Republican presidential candidate to date. The direction since then has been almost straight downhill.

The 2006-2007 Immigration Debate and 2008 Presidential Campaign

The debate over President Bush's immigration reform proposal, and its ultimate demise, created enormous problems for Republicans in the Hispanic community. Colorado representative Tom Tancredo, the anti-immigrant hard liner from a state with a fast-growing Hispanic population, became one of the loudest and most visible Republican voices against immigrants, legal and illegal.

In 2007 Tancredo announced his candidacy for the 2008 Republican presidential nomination, running primarily on the issue of illegal immigration. He boycotted a debate at the University of Miami because it was broadcast in Spanish. At a nationally-broadcast GOP debate at Saint Anselm College in New Hampshire, he said President Bush's immigration reform plan was "the worst piece of legislation to come down the pike in a long time." The consequences of that legislation should it pass? "They are incredible and they are disastrous . . . We are talking about something that goes to the very heart of this nation—whether or not we will actually survive as a nation."[41]

Tancredo ultimately dropped out of the presidential contest and endorsed Mitt Romney for president. By that time, the debate had become so poisonous that Hispanic Florida senator Mel Martinez, the then-chairman of the Republican National Committee, said, "Sometimes I feel like a man without a party."

Senator Martinez's reaction reflects what is obvious from focus groups of Hispanic voters: Hispanic Americans who came here legally take personally the harsh Republican voices targeting Hispanics who came here illegally. Once the debate devolves into "us versus them," legal Hispanics view

---

41. *http://www.ontheissues.org/2008/Tom_Tancredo_Immigration.htm*

themselves as under attack as well. The idea that Republicans can rip into illegal immigrants without antagonizing Hispanic voters is delusional.

Consequently it should surprise no one that the Democratic Party identification advantage among Hispanic registered voters ballooned from 21 percentage points over Republicans in 2006, before the immigration reform debate, to 39 percentage points by 2008 after the immigration bill collapsed.

Party Identification of Hispanic Voters: 2002-2014

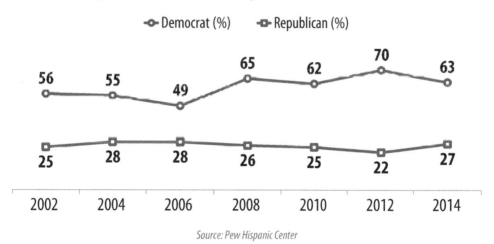

Source: Pew Hispanic Center

Figure 7-1

2012 Presidential Campaign

The image Republicans presented to Hispanic voters did not improve during the 2012 presidential nomination contest. During the course of the presidential primaries Mitt Romney:

- Hammered noted liberal Texas governor Rick Perry at a GOP debate in Florida for a law that was overwhelmingly passed by the Republican legislature to give in-state tuition at Texas public colleges and universities to children of undocumented immigrants who were brought to America as young children;[42]

- Said while campaigning in Iowa that he would veto the DREAM Act to allow those children to become citizens if they graduated from college,[43] and he declined to endorse Florida senator Marco Rubio's alternate version;

- Famously promoted "self-deportation" for undocumented Hispanics during a Florida debate,[44] which Hispanic citizens interpreted as making life so miserable for all Hispanics that they would want to leave the country.

Nor was Mitt Romney the only Republican driving Hispanics into the waiting arms of Democrats in 2012.

- Presidential candidate Herman Cain, who at one point led primary polls for the Republican nomination, said at a Tennessee political rally: "When I'm in charge, we're going to have a fence. It's going to be 20 feet high. It's going to have barbed wire on the top. It's going to be electrified. And there's going to be a sign on the other side saying 'it will kill you— Warning.'"[45]

- A Kansas Republican state representative said that the state should consider controlling illegal immigration the same way it uses helicopters and gunmen to shoot and kill wild pigs: "It looks like to me that if shooting these immigrating feral

42. http://www.foxnews.com/politics/2011/09/22/fox-news-google-gop-2012-presidential-debate/

43. http://thecaucus.blogs.nytimes.com/2011/12/31/romney-says-he-would-veto-the-dream-act/

44. http://www.cbsnews.com/news/romney-on-immigration-im-for-self-deportation/

45. http://thecaucus.blogs.nytimes.com/2011/10/15/cain-proposes-electrified-border-fence/

hogs works, maybe we have found a (solution) to our illegal immigration problem. "[46]

- Ohio Republican congressional candidate Samuel Wurzelbacher, of "Joe the Plumber" fame, said: "How many congressmen or people running for Congress have you heard [say], put a fence up and start shooting? None? Well you heard it here first. Put troops on the border and start shooting, I bet that solves our immigration problem real quick."[47]

The last two examples provide an object lesson for all Republicans. In the internet age, any elected official or any candidate *at any level* can make a remark that will damage not only their candidacy but also those of their fellow Republicans throughout the country. Democrats, and their allies in the media, will amplify any intemperate remark. The internet and YouTube place a special burden on all candidates to be careful and judicious in their public remarks.

Of course more responsible Republican voices condemned these remarks. And of course the Republicans who uttered them often passed them off as "jokes." But the damage was done. Talk show hosts on Spanish-language radio and TV captured the comments and fanned the flames. Republicans who made those comments then became the face of the Republican Party to many Hispanics who listen to Spanish-language media. And because so few Republicans speak Spanish, the party never even saw it coming.

---

46. *http://thinkprogress.org/politics/2011/03/14/150565/kansas-gop-shooting-helicoptors/*

47. *http://www.rawstory.com/rs/2012/08/14/joe-the-plumber-calls-to-start-shooting-immigrants-at-the-border/*

The political consequences were utterly predictable. Mitt Romney received the lowest percentage of the Hispanic vote of any Republican presidential candidate in a two-candidate contest since Watergate. (In 1992 and 1996, Republican nominees received lower percentages, but the vote was split three ways with Ross Perot.)

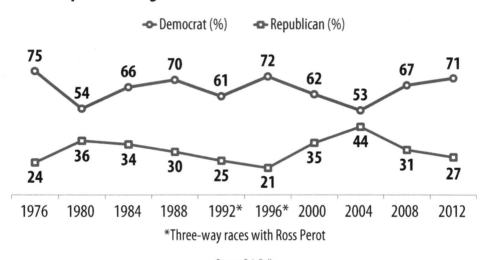

Hispanic Voting for Presidential Candidates: 1976-2012

Democrat (%)   Republican (%)

Three-way races with Ross Perot

Source: Exit Polls

Figure 7-2

Post-election surveys showed that majorities of Hispanics who voted in the 2012 election in key swing states of Florida, Colorado, New Mexico, and Nevada did not think the Republican Party "respects the values and concerns of the Hispanic community." They see the Democrats completely differently—as the party that cares about their values and concerns.

Hispanic Views of Republican Party in Four States

"Regardless of how you typically vote, do you think that the Republican Party respects the values and concerns of the Hispanic community?"

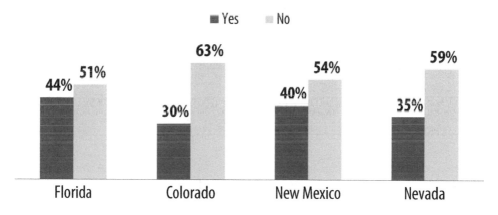

Source: Resurgent Republic / North Star Opinion Research, November 28 - December 7, 2012

Figure 7-3

On the other hand, Hispanics have a very different view of the Democratic Party.

Hispanic Views of Democratic Party in Four States

"Regardless of how you typically vote, do you think that the Democratic Party respects the values and concerns of the Hispanic community?"

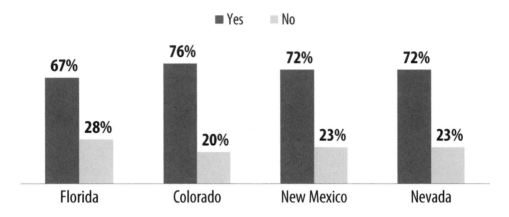

Source: Resurgent Republic / North Star Opinion Research, November 28 - December 7, 2012

Figure 7–4

Overwhelming majorities of Hispanic voters in those four states believed the phrase "supports legal immigration" better describes the Democratic Party than the Republican Party. Substantial majorities, on the other hand, believe the phrase "is anti-immigrant" better describes Republicans. Clearly Republican rhetoric has been perceived in the Hispanic community as not just anti-*illegal* immigrant, but anti-immigrant, period.

Hispanic Views of Which Party Supports Legal Immigration in Four States

"Now I would like to read you a list of phrases. For each one, would you please tell me if that phrase better describes the Republican Party or the Democratic Party—Supports legal immigration."

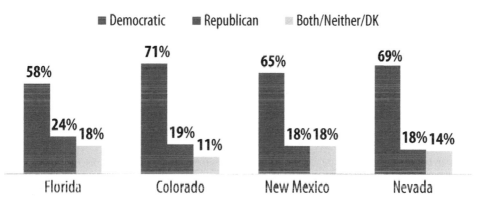

Source: Resurgent Republic / North Star Opinion Research, November 28 December 7, 2012

Figure 7-5

Hispanic Views of Which Party is Anti-Immigrant in Four States

"Now I would like to read you a list of phrases. For each one, would you please tell me if that phrase better describes the Republican Party or the Democratic Party—Is anti-immigrant."

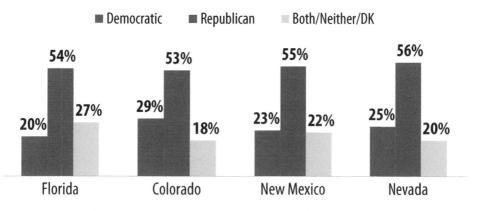

Source: Resurgent Republic / North Star Opinion Research, November 28 - December 7, 2012

Figure 7-6

The 2013-2014 Immigration Debate

Unfortunately derogatory comments about Hispanics from Republican candidates and elected officials did not end in 2012.

During the 2013 immigration reform debate, Iowa Republican congressman Steve King offered the following description of undocumented Hispanic young people: "For every one who's a valedictorian, there's another 100 out there that weigh 130 pounds and they've got calves the size of cantaloupes because they're hauling 75 pounds of marijuana across the desert."[48]

In 2014 Republican congressman and Air Force veteran Jeff Denham proposed a bill to grant legal status to young undocumented immigrants who volunteer to serve in the military. That proposal, essentially a "DREAM Act" for military veterans, was the only portion of the DREAM Act that Mitt Romney supported during the 2012 campaign. As detailed below, the proposal is supported by 83 percent of all American voters, as well as 80 percent of Republican voters.

Congressman King's reaction? "As soon as they raise their hand and say, 'I'm unlawfully present in the United States,' we're not going to take your oath into the military, but we're going to take your deposition and we have a bus for you to Tijuana."[49]

Imagine the reaction of Hispanics who are American citizens when they read comments like those from Congressman King. A Hispanic youngster raised in the United States volunteers to put his or her life on the line to protect America, and a prominent Republican congressman's reaction is to

---

48. *http://www.politico.com/story/2013/07/joe-garcia-steve-king-94630. html#ixzz2ZxaAl84V*

49. *http://www.nytimes.com/2014/04/05/us/politics/new-push-on-immigration-bill-causes-gop-rift.html?hpw&rref=politics*

threaten to put him on a bus to Tijuana? Is it any wonder that Hispanics view Republicans as "the anti-immigrant party"?

The hole Republicans have dug for themselves in the Hispanic community over the past eight years is very deep. The most important step now is to stop digging. How Republicans handle the immigration reform debate going forward will determine whether the digging has stopped and climbing out has begun.

Immigration Reform

So how do Republicans handle immigration reform that is consistent with Republican principles, is true to American ideals, and gains rather than loses Hispanic support?

First, passing immigration reform will not solve every Republicans problem in the Hispanic community. The trouble goes beyond immigration, and has gotten significantly worse over the last eight years. To be competitive among Hispanics, Republicans need to adopt a very different tone toward Hispanics, and demonstrate over a period of years that they have better answers than the Democrats to creating paths of opportunity to achieve the American dream.

But supporting fair and reasonable immigration reform is the first step on that journey. While immigration is not the most important issue among Hispanics (jobs and the economy lead by a mile), it is a threshold issue that sends symbolic signals to all Hispanics, legal and illegal. Reflexively screaming "amnesty" to any proposal, no matter how reasonable, is exactly the wrong reaction to immigration reform proposals. Focus groups of Hispanic voters make clear that if Republicans are not reasonably sympathetic to the plight of Hispanic families and the difficulty many face with documentation, they will never listen to anything Republicans say on any other issue.

So where to begin? First recognize that the vast majority of Americans believe *legal* immigration has helped rather than hurt this country. Calls for reducing legal immigration, as anti-immigration groups like Numbers USA and the Federation for American Immigration Reform want to do, automatically place the proponent outside the mainstream of American political thinking. They also violate the foundational principles of a country that has the Statue of Liberty greeting visitors in New York harbor.

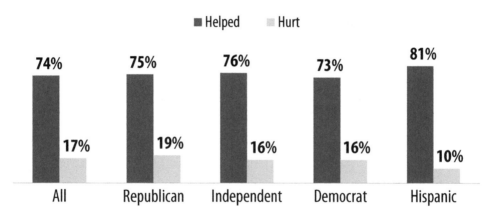

Has Legal Immigration Helped or Hurt America

"Overall, would you say legal immigration has helped or hurt America?"

Source: North Star Opinion Research, April 10-12, 2012

Figure 7-7

A majority of Americans believe illegal immigration is a major problem facing the country. While more Republicans view it as a major problem than other groups do, a plurality of all groups sees illegal immigration as a major problem, *including* Hispanics. This is an issue that begs for attention and resolution.

Is Illegal Immigration a Problem

"Would you say illegal immigration is a major problem, a minor problem, or not a real problem in America today?"

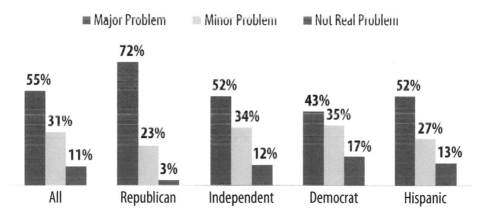

Source: North Star Opinion Research, April 10-12, 2012

Figure 7-8

Despite the overwhelming agreement that illegal immigration is a problem, the vast majority of Americans believe that it is impossible to deport most illegal immigrants back to their home countries. Americans, including Republicans, have come to accept, however reluctantly, that most undocumented immigrants are here to stay.

Is It Possible To Deport Most Illegal Immigrants

"As you probably know, there are somewhere between ten and twelve million undocumented or illegal immigrants who are living in America. Do you think it is possible to deport most of them back to their home countries, or do you think most of them are here to stay?"

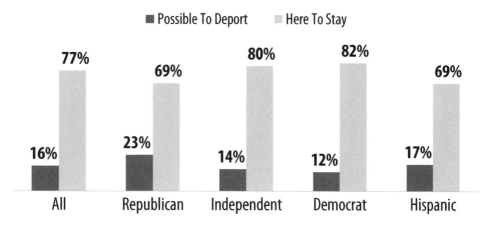

Source: North Star Opinion Research, April 10-12, 2012

Figure 7–9

An Immigration Reform Plan

Since Americans support legal immigration, view illegal immigration as a major problem, and think most illegal immigrants are here to stay, what kind of immigration reform plan will Americans support? The task is extraordinarily complex with many pitfalls, but the fundamental principles proposed by Republicans in both the Senate[50] and House of Representatives[51] enjoy widespread popular support:

- Recognize that the current immigration system is irretrievably broken, and is not working for our economy, for our national security, or for the millions of people affected by the broken system;

- Aggressively strengthen border security with fences, electronic monitoring, and more border guards so that immigration reform will not lead to another wave of illegal immigration;

- Institute a visa tracking system to ensure that those who came to America legally on temporary visas actually leave when their visas expire (40 percent of undocumented immigrants arrived here legally but overstayed their visas);

- Create an efficient electronic employment verification system that will prevent identity theft and end the hiring of unauthorized workers;

- Establish a functional temporary-worker program for admitting future workers to serve the nation's workforce needs in agriculture and other fields that do not displace American workers;

- Reform the legal immigration system so that it is driven by the needs of our economy for both high-skilled and low-skilled workers, rather than by reunifying extended families;

---

50. *http://www.nytimes.com/2013/01/28/us/politics/senators-agree-on-blueprint-for-immigration.html?pagewanted=all87*

51. *http://www.nytimes.com/2014/01/31/us/politics/text-of-republicans-principles-on-immigration.html?_r=0*

- Develop a plan that would allow undocumented young people brought to this country illegally by their parents to gain legal status and, eventually, citizenship;

- Create a tough and lengthy path to legalization for undocumented adult immigrants without criminal records who currently live in the U.S. That path requires background checks, fines, current and back taxes, learning English, denial of government benefits during the waiting period, and, for those who ultimately want to apply for citizenship, going to the back of the line.

Public opinion supports each of those principles.

Support Among All Voters and Republican Voters for Various Immigration Reform Proposals

"Would you please tell me if you strongly support, somewhat support, somewhat oppose, or strongly oppose each of the following policy options:"

■ Support ▪ Oppose

Allowing children of undocumented immigrants who have been here for years to obtain legal residency status after their honorable discharge from service in the U.S. military

Allowing undocumented immigrants who have been here for years to obtain legal residency status if they pay a fine, have a job, and learn English

Setting up a temporary-worker program where people would come to America legally for a limited time to work in areas like agriculture, after which they would be required to return to their home countries

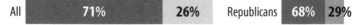

Allowing children of undocumented immigrants who have been here for years to obtain legal residency status if they graduate from college

Source: North Star Opinion Research, April 10-12, 2012

Figure 7-10

Americans have developed a consensus about how to handle the case of young undocumented adults brought to the country as young children—the "DREAMers." The following question tests an actual case:

Let me give you an example of an undocumented immigrant and have you tell me what you think should be done in this case. Suzanna was brought to America illegally by her mother when she was two years old. She performed well in school, and became valedictorian of her high school class. She has been admitted to an Ivy League university and offered a full scholarship. She has also received a letter from the federal government telling her she is going to be deported. Which statement comes closer to your view:

a) It's a heartbreaking story, but the law is the law and Suzanna should be deported. Allowing undocumented immigrants to stay in America is amnesty, and we should never adopt amnesty no matter what the circumstances. Allowing her to stay would encourage other parents to bring their children here illegally and make the illegal immigration problem worse.

b) Suzanna should not be deported. Instead she should be allowed the opportunity to earn legal status, and when she finishes college she should be given a work visa that allows her to become a legal resident. After five years of being a legal resident, she can then apply for citizenship and wait in line like any other immigrant if she wants to. Deporting people like Suzanna is unjust and hurts our country. Besides, to what country would we deport her? America is her home.

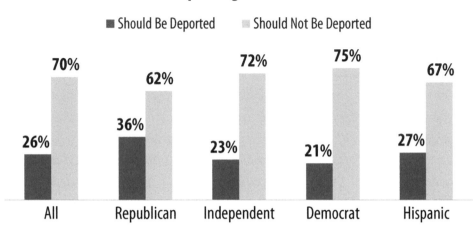

Deporting Suzanna

■ Should Be Deported   ▨ Should Not Be Deported

	All	Republican	Independent	Democrat	Hispanic
Should Be Deported	26%	36%	23%	21%	27%
Should Not Be Deported	70%	62%	72%	75%	67%

Source: North Star Opinion Research, April 10-12, 2012

Figure 7-11

Interestingly, changing Suzanna's record to performing adequately in school, graduating near the middle of her high school class, and being admitted to a local community college, instead of performing well in school, being valedictorian of her high school class, and being admitted to an Ivy League college, has almost no effect on Americans' views about the outcome. Overwhelming majorities believe she should be allowed to earn legal status and not be deported, regardless of whether her record is average or outstanding.

Dealing with the eleven million undocumented immigrants currently in the country poses the greatest challenge in finding a solution to the immigration problem, but even on that principle a broad consensus exists in public opinion on about the way forward.

Americans overwhelmingly support an intermediate step between illegality and full citizenship. Legal residency status allows undocumented immigrants to come out of the shadows, but not jump ahead of those waiting in line to enter the country legally.

Is Earned Legal Status a Good or Bad Idea

"Some people have proposed allowing undocumented or illegal immigrants with no criminal record to earn legal status with a work visa if they meet certain criteria. Earned legal status would not make them citizens, but would allow them to come out of the shadows and stay in America if they have a job. They could apply for citizenship and wait in line like any other immigrant if they desired. In general, do you think earned legal status with a work visa is a good idea or a bad idea for dealing with undocumented immigrants with no criminal record?"

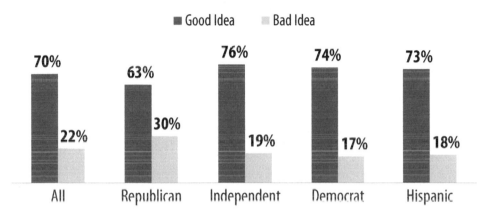

Source: North Star Opinion Research, April 10-12, 2012

Figure 7-12

The vast majority of Americans, including an overwhelming majority of Republicans, supports allowing undocumented immigrants to gain legal residency status if they serve in the military or graduate from college, or pay a fine, have a job, and learn English.

A minority of Republicans—between 25 and 30 percent—opposes a path to citizenship under any circumstances. They are loud and intense and attempt to intimidate many elected officials. But they offer no workable solution for the problem. No reasonable person believes we are going to round up and deport eleven million undocumented people, many of whom have lived here for years, and whose families are interwoven with both the documented and undocumented. Mass deportation is not going to happen.

Alternate Scenario #1: It's Hopeless

Some conservative analysts utterly reject the argument that Republicans should embrace immigration reform. They believe any effort short of deportation will lead to a flood of new illegal immigrants. Those who believe Republicans should stand resolutely against immigration reform paint three different scenarios.

The first is "It's hopeless because Hispanics will always vote for Democrats so we should not even try."[52] These analysts claim that Hispanics come from countries with activist governments, so they support big government solutions and Democratic arguments. Legalizing illegal immigrants will just flood the Democratic voter rolls with new recruits. In its crasser form, proponents of this point of view argue that non-white voters are basically socialists, and demographic trends mean America is on an inevitable downward slide into socialism.[53]

"It's hopeless" is an argument for people who do not really believe in their own principles.

Those who make this argument believe the center-right governing philosophy is doomed. They offer no answer to the coming demographic changes other than hand-wringing. And they do not really believe in the universal

---

52. *http://www.nationalreview.com/corner/332916/why-hispanics-dont-vote-republicans-heather-mac-donald*

53. See the last ten minutes of this panel at CPAC: *http://www.c-span.org/video/?318148-11/2014-conservative-political-action-conference-demographics-panel*

appeal of free markets, limited government, and individual liberty. Or they apparently believe that those principles only work for white people.

Fortunately, their argument is wrong. Yes, an earlier chart shows that Hispanics have voted more often for Democratic than Republican candidates for president since exit polling began. But the chart also demonstrates great variation in Hispanic voting, from George W. Bush's 44 percent in 2004 to Mitt Romney's 27 percent in 2012. That difference has enormous implications for swing state results and electoral college math, implications that will only grow in the future as Hispanics become a more significant portion of the electorate.

Moreover, it is simply not true that Hispanics will never vote for Republican candidates in significant numbers. Numerous Republican candidates who have reached out to the Hispanic community have won many Hispanic votes in recent years. A few examples:

- Not only did George W. Bush win 44 percent of the Hispanic vote nationally in his 2004 reelection campaign, he won 49 percent of Texas Hispanics[54] and 56 percent of Florida Hispanic voters that year.[55]

- Senator Mel Martinez won 60 percent of Hispanics in Florida in his 2004 U.S. Senate campaign.[56]

- Senator Marco Rubio won 55 percent of Hispanics in Florida in his 2010 U.S. Senate campaign.[57]

---

54. *http://www.politifact.com/texas/statements/2013/jun/04/karl-rove/karl-rove-says-republicans-running-texas-draw-40-p/*

55. *http://www.cnn.com/ELECTION/2004/pages/results/states/FL/P/00/epolls.0.html*

56. *http://www.cnn.com/ELECTION/2004/pages/results/states/FL/S/01/epolls.0.html*

57. *http://www.cnn.com/ELECTION/2010/results/polls/#FLS01p1*

- Senator John Cornyn won 48 percent of Hispanic voters in Texas in his 2014 reelection campaign.[58]

Republican candidates *can* win significant numbers of Hispanic votes, but they have to try.

Alternate Scenario #2: The "Missing White Voters"

Other opponents of immigration reform are not so fatalistic. They believe Republicans can be competitive in the future, not by winning more votes among Hispanics, but by increasing the number and share of white votes, by finding "the missing white voters" who did not vote in 2012.

Some analysts argue that fewer white voters voted in 2012 than in 2008. They make the case that they are largely blue-collar white voters, the kinds of people who voted for Ross Perot in 1992 and 1996. They argue that mobilizing these voters points the way to a more competitive future for Republican presidential candidates without having to gain more Hispanic votes.[59]

The following table shows the number of votes in the presidential elections from 2000 to 2012. Using exit poll results from the percentage of the electorate that is white, and the percent of the white vote for the Republican candidate, we can construct estimates of the total number of white voters in each year and the number of white votes won by the Republican candidate.

---

58. *http://www.cnn.com/election/2014/results/state/TX/senate#exit-polls*

59. *http://www.realclearpolitics.com/articles/2013/06/21/the_case_of_the_missing_white_voters_revisited_118893.html*

Votes for President by Race: 2000-2012

	2000	2004	2008	2012	Change '08-'12
Votes for Rep candidate	50,462,412	62,039,572	59,950,323	60,932,235	981,912
Votes for Dem candidate	51,009,810	59,027,115	69,499,428	65,917,258	-3,582,170
Votes for other candidates	3,953,763	1,236,903	2,023,954	2,382,613	358,659
Total number votes	105,425,985	122,303,590	131,473,705	129,232,106	-2,241,599
% of white electorate (exit polls)	81%	77%	74%	72%	-2 points
Est. Nº of white votes	85,395,048	94,173,764	97,290,542	93,047,116	-4,243,425
Est. Nº of non-white votes	20,030,937	28,129,826	34,183,163	36,184,990	2,001,826
% of white votes won by Rep	54%	58%	55%	59%	4 points
Est. Nº of white votes won by Rep	46,113,326	54,620,783	53,509,798	54,897,799	1,388,001

Source: USElectionAtlas.org

Figure 7-13

The number of white voters did drop from 2008 to 2012 by about 4.2 million. We have already argued in Chapter 1 that part of the reason for Romney's loss was his relatively weak performance among northern white voters, especially those in the upper Midwest. It makes sense that the white voters who did not show up in 2012 were blue-collar voters who were not attracted to Barack Obama but who could never warm up to the patrician demeanor of Mitt Romney. The chart also makes even more critical points:

- Romney won more white votes than any Republican nominee in this century, including more white votes than George W. Bush won during his reelection in 2004.

- Romney won a larger share of white votes than any Republican nominee this century.

- Even if all the "missing white voters" had showed up, and every single one had voted for Romney, he still would have lost the election.

Constructing a scenario where Republican presidential candidates can succeed in the future by gaining more white voters without gaining a larger share of Hispanic voters requires a series of highly tenuous assumptions. The most tenuous of all is that Republican candidates can garner 70 percent of the white vote.

That assumption strains credulity. No Republican presidential candidate in the history of exit polling has *ever* achieved that level of the white vote, even Ronald Reagan in his landslide 49-state sweep in 1984.

The chart in Chapter 1 shows that Mitt Romney only achieved 70 percent of the white vote in the relatively small, racially-polarized states of Alabama and Mississippi. (Romney probably won that high a percentage of the white vote in heavily Mormon Utah, but no exit polls are available for that state in 2012.) In the vast majority of states, including the critical swing states of the upper Midwest, Romney did not even reach 60 percent among whites. A very conservative candidate who can win 70 percent of the white vote in the Deep South would struggle to gain even 50 percent of the white vote in the more populous and liberal states in the Northeast and far West.

The idea that a Republican presidential candidate in the future can consistently win 70 percent of the white vote nationally is a pipe dream.

The "missing white voters" explanation for why Republican presidential candidates have not performed better is reminiscent of the excuses some Democratic analysts offered for why their candidates lost so consistently during the 1980s. The reason, we were told, was the large number of non-voters who, if they had voted, would have supported the Democratic nominee. Democrats did not need to change their message or the types of candidates they nominated. All they needed to do was find these elusive "non-voters" and get them to the polls. It never happened.

The fundamental problem with the "missing white voters" strategy is that it denies the obvious historical trends laid out in Chapter 2. In every single presidential election since 1996, white voters have constituted a lower percentage of the electorate than the election before. There is no reason to believe that trend has stopped—if anything the trend is accelerating.

Relying on "missing white voters" for future Republican presidential victories is not a strategy. It is an excuse, an excuse to avoid confronting the very real problems facing the Republican Party in a 21st century presidential electorate.

Alternate Scenario #3: Immigration Reform Doesn't Matter

Others argue that Republicans can win more Hispanic votes if they nominate candidates more sympathetic to Hispanic concerns, even if they oppose immigration reform. They argue that immigration reform is far from the most important issue in the Hispanic community, and candidates who resonate on jobs, health care, and opportunity can gain traction among Hispanic voters. In this view, candidates who use the right tone, reach out to the Hispanic community, and advertise aggressively on Hispanic media will garner more Hispanic voters than Romney was able to achieve regardless of whether other Republicans support reform.

This is the most plausible of the alternative scenarios, but it all depends on the candidates. A candidate who ardently opposes immigration reform will not resonate in the Hispanic community for reasons discussed above.

Republican candidates who support immigration reform may be able to perform well among Hispanics despite their party if they separate themselves from the anti-immigrant voices within their party. If congressional Republicans are perceived by Hispanics as blocking immigration reform, it places an extra burden on any future Republican candidates who hope to perform well among Hispanic voters.

The Way Forward

Barack Obama issued an executive order on November 20, 2014, unilaterally legalizing about five million illegal immigrants. In the wake of an electoral shellacking only two weeks earlier, the action was provocative and infuriating to Republicans across the land. Obama's defiance in the face of a massive defeat is truly maddening. Even though a dozen new Republican senators were elected on November 4, Obama did not even wait until they were sworn in before poking a stick in their eye.

The challenge for Republicans is how to respond to this provocation without digging an even deeper hole with Hispanics. Obama has certainly made passing a long-term legislative solution to our broken immigration system more difficult. Nevertheless, the most productive response is to make the executive order moot by passing a bill, or a set of bills, that reforms the broken immigration system.

The building blocks of that reform are contained in the bipartisan comprehensive immigration reform bill that passed the Senate 68 to 32 in 2013. While even its supporters admit that that bill was far from perfect and reflected the messy compromises required to get a bill passed, it did make a serious effort to address the fundamental principles outlined by Republican congressional leaders.

The House did not take up that bill for a year and a half, leading Obama to issue his executive order. The House appears inclined to pass a series of bills rather than one comprehensive bill, which will work equally well as long as those bills address all important components of serious reform. But not acting at all plays into the hands of Obama and the Democrats, who are actively working to paint Republicans as the arch enemy of America's fastest growing minority group.

Dos and Don'ts

Following are some dos and don'ts for Republicans who hope to perform better at the ballot box among Hispanic voters:

- **Do** aggressively recruit, support, and promote attractive Hispanic candidates who share Republican principles. Republicans are actually ahead of Democrats in that task today. Florida senator Marco Rubio, New Mexico governor Susanna Martinez, and Nevada governor Brian Sandoval are among the attractive Hispanic Republican candidates with broad-based appeal. Together they constitute a far more appealing class of high-ranking Hispanic candidates than anything Democrats can currently offer.

- **Do** develop sophisticated campaigns to appeal to Hispanics that include Spanish-language advertising to run on Spanish-language television and radio stations. That advertising needs to be much more than simply Spanish translations of English-language ads. The 2012 Obama campaign developed an entire television campaign focused on the concerns of Hispanics, a completely different campaign than that run on English-language television.

- **Do** encourage Hispanic and non-Hispanic Republican candidates to learn Spanish. Not many Republicans realize it, but Barack Obama speaks the language, at least well enough to cut a television ad in Spanish that reached out to the Hispanic community and asked for their votes.

- **Do** respect the values and concerns of the Hispanic community. Many Hispanics live in fear of a knock on the door, of a deportation order for a family member who is undocumented while others, who are here legally, will be left behind. Republican candidates need to be sensitive to the particular pressures and challenges facing many in the Hispanic community.

On the other hand, here are a few don'ts:

- **Do not** argue for immigration reform using a political calculus, saying it is the only way for Republicans to be politically competitive in the future. While the statement is true, using a political rationale is only persuasive to political operatives, pundits, and activists. Voters are far more persuaded by an argument that immigration reform is good for our security, good for the economy, and good the country.

- **Do not** tolerate language or tone in any Republican candidate at any level that is harsh or demeaning to Hispanic voters. Some Republicans tell themselves that they can use any language they want when referring to undocumented immigrants without consequence among Hispanic voters. Any focus group of Hispanic voters will quickly convince them otherwise. The Party leadership and elected officials not only need to set an example of inclusive language, but need to make crystal clear that anti-Hispanic rhetoric will not be tolerated in the Republican Party.

Conclusion

Large majorities of Americans, including large majorities of Republicans, support the building blocks of fair and reasonable immigration reform. Getting out of the hole Republicans have dug in the Hispanic community requires Republican elected officials to support that effort and to lead it. Rather than cursing the darkness, reflexively screaming "amnesty," and calling for deportation of a population the size of Ohio, they need to light a candle and show the way forward on this complex issue. And they must do this in a way that solves the problem and does not doom the Republican Party to political irrelevance in the future.

Republicans can be competitive in the increasingly important Hispanic community, as so many Republican candidates have already shown. But doing so will require a new tone, a new attitude toward immigration re-form, and a renewed belief that Republican principles of individual liberty, free enterprise, limited government, personal responsibility, and expanded opportunity are attractive to *all* Americans, regardless of race, creed, or color.

There will never be a perfect time to address a seriously broken system. Doing so responsibly before the next presidential election would dem-onstrate that Republicans are serious about governing. It would also lay a foundation for the 2016 Republican presidential nominee to perform far better in the Hispanic community than in the two prior presidential elections.

There is little doubt that supporting responsible immigration reform will, in the long run, be good for the country, good for the economy, and good for the Republican Party.

★ ★ ★ **8** ★ ★ ★

OBAMACARE *and* ITS LEGACY

Few issues have consumed as much political energy since President Obama took office as reform of America's health care system. Remaking almost one-fifth of the American economy and advancing the long-time Democratic goal of government-guaranteed universal health care for all has proven to be both enormously complex and incredibly controversial. The way the Democrats passed ObamaCare—ramming it through Congress on a straight party-line vote, changing the rules along the way to get it through the Senate—ensured that congressional passage was not the end of the story, but merely one battle in a long-running fight over the future of health care in America.

Is Health Care a Right?

The roots of contemporary disagreements about health care lie in fundamental differences in the American electorate about responsibility for providing it. For years liberals have argued that health care is a "right." The concept of a "right" implies certain characteristics:

- Equality of result. If everyone has a "right" to vote, that implies that each individual has only one vote, the same number as everyone else. We would recoil against the argument that better-off Americans should be allowed to "buy" additional votes on Election Day. Similarly, if health care is a "right," then everyone should have roughly the same coverage and the same quality. Indeed, in some countries with universal health care, it is illegal for better-off citizens to go outside the state-sponsored health care system to purchase better or faster health care.

- Government control. "Rights," by definition, are regulated, interpreted, and enforced by government. Benefits that are not deemed to be "rights" are regulated by the economic sphere, and people who can afford more benefits can purchase more. So if health care is a "right," then inevitably the federal government will be deeply involved in determining what kind, what quality, and how much care each of us can receive.

- Entitlement. If health care is a "right," then every individual is entitled to receive health care regardless of their ability to pay. In other words, they are "entitled" to health care by virtue of being an American citizen. The program providing it will be an "entitlement," and everyone will get the benefit of that entitlement regardless of their circumstances.

Do Americans believe health care is a "right?" Democrats do, by a substantial margin. But Republicans believe health care is "something that citizens should be primarily responsible for providing for themselves," by more than a five-to-one margin. Independents think more like Republicans than Democrats, so that a majority of American voters believes health care is a citizen's responsibility rather than a right.

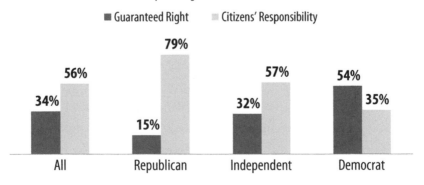

Is Health Care a Right or a Citizen's Responsibility

"In general, do you view health care as a right guaranteed to all citizens by the federal government, or is it something that citizens should be primarily responsible for providing for themselves?"

■ Guaranteed Right ▪ Citizens' Responsibility

Source: AAN / North Star Opinion Research, National Survey of Registered Voters, March 18-21, 2013

Figure 8-1

Congressional Passage of Major Health Care Initiatives

Because more Americans believe health care is a citizen's responsibility than it is a right, liberals have had difficulty passing government-run universal health care for all. So their strategy has focused on chipping away at their long-term goal by providing government-run health care group by group, passing programs for seniors in Medicare and for the poor in Medicaid.

Passage of Medicare and Medicaid did not stimulate the ongoing political warfare generated by ObamaCare, in large part because support for those was bi-partisan. Indeed, a *majority* of Republican congressmen voting supported Medicare on its passage in 1965.

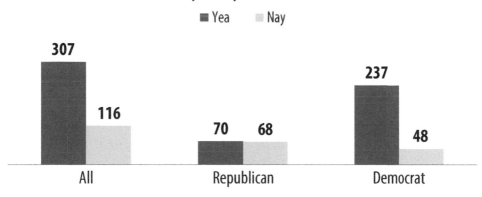

House Votes by Party for Medicare in 1965

■ Yea ■ Nay

	All	Republican	Democrat
Yea	307	70	237
Nay	116	68	48

Note: 10 House members did not vote.

Source: www.ssa.gov

Figure 8-2

Forty-three percent of Republican senators casting a vote supported Medicare as well.

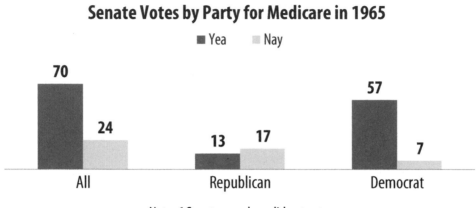

Senate Votes by Party for Medicare in 1965

Note: 6 Senate members did not vote.

Source: www.ssa.gov

Figure 8-3

In the years since its passage, Medicare has become breathtakingly popular, with 92 percent of seniors satisfied with their Medicare plan and only 6 percent dissatisfied. Obviously any changes to a program with 92 percent satisfaction need to be approached with great care.

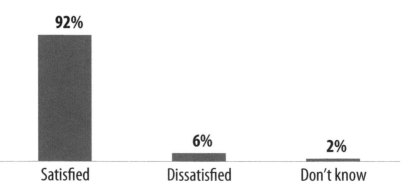

Satisfaction with Medicare Among Seniors in 2013

"Overall, how satisfied are you with your traditional Medicare plan?"

Source: AHIP / North Star Opinion Research, National Survey of Seniors, February 6-11, 2013

Figure 8-4

In 2003, Congress passed an expansion to Medicare by adding a prescription drug benefit known as Part D. The proposal explicitly brought private health insurance plans into the program by setting up competition among the various plans for the business of Medicare recipients. Because the expansion was promoted by President George W. Bush, and because it involved private companies in the popular public program, Democrats, led by Speaker of the House Nancy Pelosi, fought the plan. Consequently congressional votes were more partisan than in the original adoption of Medicare, but some Democrats in both the House and Senate voted for the Medicare prescription drug benefit.

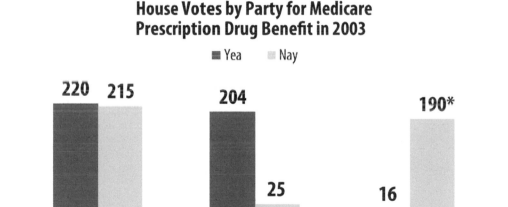

House Votes by Party for Medicare Prescription Drug Benefit in 2003

Bernie Sanders (I-VT) voted with Democrats.

Source: www.govtrack.us

Figure 8-5

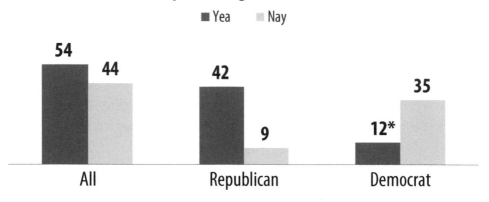

Senate Votes by Party for Medicare Prescription Drug Benefit in 2003

■ Yea   ▨ Nay

54 **44**	**42** **9**	**12*** **35**
All	Republican	Democrat

*Jim Jeffords (I-VT) voted with Democrats.

Note: 2 Senate members did not vote.

Source: www.govtrack.us

Figure 8-6

The irony of Medicare Part D is that it has become an orphan success story, a successful government program that no one wants to own. Republicans won't claim it because it established a new entitlement; Democrats won't claim it because it was a Republican idea. But the competition at the heart of the prescription drug benefit drove costs down to two-thirds of initial estimates. Merely three years after passage, two-thirds of seniors thought it was a good idea.

Do Seniors Think Medicare Prescription Drug Benefit is a Good or Bad Idea

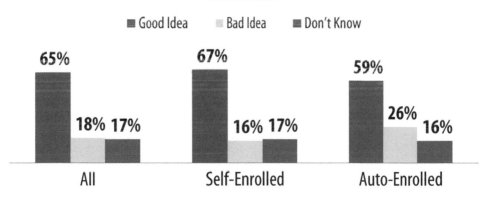

"Overall, do you think passing the Medicare prescription drug plan was a good idea or a bad idea?"

■ Good Idea   ■ Bad Idea   ■ Don't Know

	All	Self-Enrolled	Auto-Enrolled
Good Idea	65%	67%	59%
Bad Idea	18%	16%	26%
Don't Know	17%	17%	16%

Source: AHIP / North Star Opinion Research, National Survey of Seniors Enrolled in Medicare Part D, September 8-10, 2006

Figure 8-7

But passage of ObamaCare in 2010 was a completely different story from passage of either Medicare or the Medicare prescription drug benefit. Democrats enjoyed an overwhelming majority in the House and a filibuster-proof majority in the Senate. They could have reached across the aisle to incorporate Republican ideas and garner at least some Republican support, especially in the Senate, but their attitude was "We've got the votes. We're going to do what we want." And they certainly did, cramming their preferred bill through the Congress *without a single Republican vote* in either the House or the Senate.

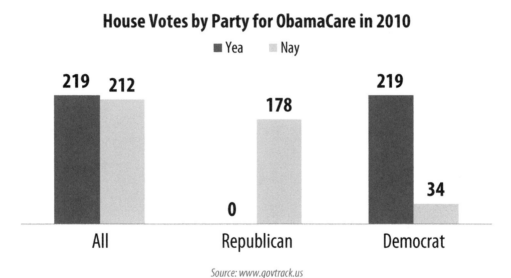

Figure 8-8

Senate Votes by Party for ObamaCare in 2010

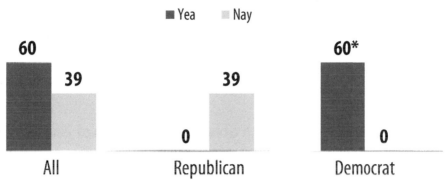

■ Yea   ■ Nay

60		**60***
39	**39**	
	0	**0**
All	Republican	Democrat

*Joe Lieberman (I-CT) and Bernie Sanders (I-VT) voted with Democrats.
Note: 1 Senate member did not vote.

Source: www.govtrack.us

Figure 8-9

After the Senate passed the bill, Republican Scott Brown won Senator Ted Kennedy's seat in Massachusetts, reducing the number of Democratic seats to one below the filibuster threshold of sixty. So the Democratic leadership in the Senate changed the rules, and passed the final bill under rules established for budget bills with fifty-six Democratic votes and no Republican votes.

The result was eminently predictable: a continuing fight over implementing ObamaCare in which congressional passage was merely one battle in the long war. America did not see lingering battles after prior health care reform initiatives because they were not crammed through Congress in bitter, straight party-line votes. But the way ObamaCare was passed ensured ongoing partisan warfare.

Initial Public Attitudes About ObamaCare

Democrats passed ObamaCare over the objection of the American electorate—more people opposed than supported the bill throughout congressional debate and during the first three years after its passage. But, up
until the middle of 2013, opposition only surpassed support by a single-
digit margin—the following chart shows a typical pattern.

Support or Oppose ObamaCare in March of 2013

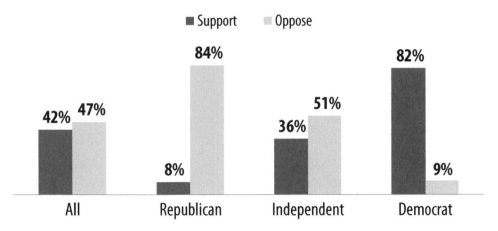

"Do you support or oppose the health care reform law that passed in 2010, also known
as the Affordable Care Act or ObamaCare?"

Source: AAN / North Star Opinion Research, National Survey of Registered Voters, March 18-21, 2013

Figure 8-10

Why has ObamaCare never been able to generate majority support? One
reason was clear even as the bill was being debated. Overwhelmingly the
top priority for voters in health care reform is *making health care more affordable*. Improving the quality of care and covering more of the uninsured
lagged far behind as priorities.

Top Priority for Health Care

"Which of the following do you think should be the top priority for health care in America today: improving the quality of health care, making health care more affordable, or covering the uninsured?"

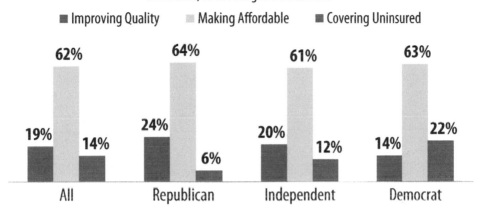

■ Improving Quality   ■ Making Affordable   ■ Covering Uninsured

Source: Crossroads GPS / North Star Opinion Research, National Survey of Registered Voters, June 2-5, 2013

Figure 8-11

Democratic strategists, of course, saw the same numbers. Why else would they name the bill "The Affordable Care Act?" The problem, of course, was that affordability was not the bill's top priority—it was expanding coverage to those without it. And the American voters figured that out. The only people who think the law will accomplish its goals are those who think covering the uninsured is the top priority. Indeed, those who think the top priority is making health care more affordable think "The Affordable Care Act" will make affordability *worse*, not better.

Does ObamaCare Help or Hurt Your Top Priority

"Thinking specifically about that top priority, would you say the health care reform law passed in 2010 helps achieve that priority, makes things worse, or has no effect on that priority?"

■ Helps Achieve　　■ Makes Worse　　■ No Effect

Source: Crossroads GPS / North Star Opinion Research, National Survey of Registered Voters, June 2-5, 2013

Figure 8-12

Of course, making health care less affordable was not the only ObamaCare problem in the view of the American electorate. Democrats pulled off a truly stunning achievement when they passed a piece of legislation that American voters believe will raise their health care costs, their premiums, their taxes, and the federal deficit, while simultaneously hurting the quality of care.

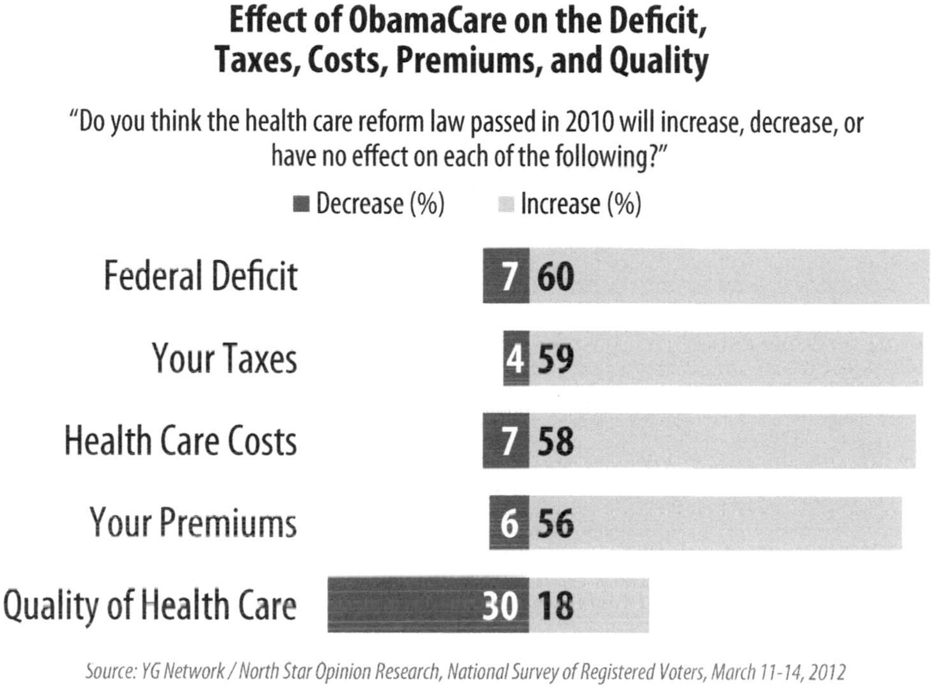

Effect of ObamaCare on the Deficit, Taxes, Costs, Premiums, and Quality

"Do you think the health care reform law passed in 2010 will increase, decrease, or have no effect on each of the following?"

■ Decrease (%)　　■ Increase (%)

	Decrease	Increase
Federal Deficit	7	60
Your Taxes	4	59
Health Care Costs	7	58
Your Premiums	6	56
Quality of Health Care	30	18

Source: YG Network / North Star Opinion Research, National Survey of Registered Voters, March 11-14, 2012

Figure 8-13

During the course of debate President Obama and his Democratic allies offered many glowing promises about the impending legislation:

The plan will not add one dime to the federal budget deficit.

The plan will lower health insurance premiums for the average family by $2,500 per year.

The plan will lower health care costs for individuals, businesses, and the federal government.

The plan will not require cuts in Medicare.

The plan will not increase taxes for anyone who earns under $250,000 a year.

The plan will not lead to a doctor shortage, rationing, or harm the quality of care.

If you like your current health plan, you will be able to keep it.

The problem is that, only two years later, a substantial majority of Americans believed all of those claims to be false, except one.

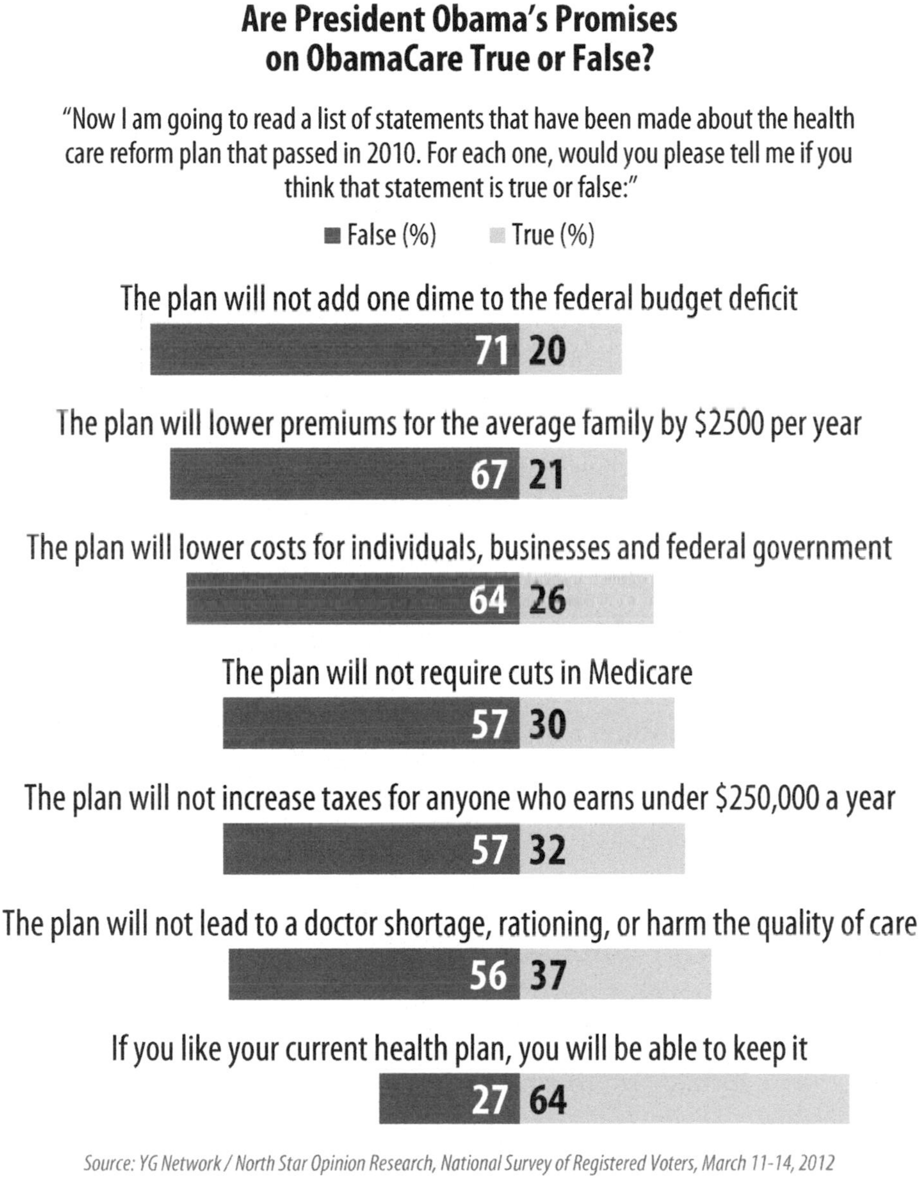

Are President Obama's Promises on ObamaCare True or False?

"Now I am going to read a list of statements that have been made about the health care reform plan that passed in 2010. For each one, would you please tell me if you think that statement is true or false:"

■ False (%)　　■ True (%)

The plan will not add one dime to the federal budget deficit

71 20

The plan will lower premiums for the average family by $2500 per year

67 21

The plan will lower costs for individuals, businesses and federal government

64 26

The plan will not require cuts in Medicare

57 30

The plan will not increase taxes for anyone who earns under $250,000 a year

57 32

The plan will not lead to a doctor shortage, rationing, or harm the quality of care

56 37

If you like your current health plan, you will be able to keep it

27 64

Source: YG Network / North Star Opinion Research, National Survey of Registered Voters, March 11-14, 2012

Figure 8–14

The one claim voters believed, of course, is the now-infamous promise that "If you like your current health plan, you will be able to keep it." As a famous politician once said, "Oops!"

So if the American electorate held such overwhelmingly negative views about the likely effects of ObamaCare, why wasn't opposition to the law also overwhelming during its passage and the initial years thereafter? Why didn't 65 percent or 75 percent of American voters oppose the law, rather than opposition in the upper 40s?

One answer may be that during the first three years Americans had not yet experienced the reality of the law. Their views were necessarily based on differing predictions about what would likely happen, frequently offered by partisans strongly trying to support their party's position.

Another answer is that, while most Americans with coverage are satisfied with their health insurance plans, health insurance companies as a whole are not popular. Denial of coverage because of pre-existing conditions, cancelled coverage, and denial of benefits created substantial antipathy toward health insurance companies. Democrats used that to their advantage to generate support for ObamaCare. Whenever Republicans raise problems with ObamaCare, Democrats immediately charge that Republicans want to put health insurance companies back in charge. And it works.

Consider the following two arguments about ObamaCare, the case against written by our Republican firm, and the case for written by Democratic pollster Stan Greenberg.

> **The Republican candidate** *says ObamaCare is bad for America. Our number one problem is the cost of care, and this law will raise, not lower, our health care costs. It will increase our health insurance premiums, increase our taxes, increase the deficit, and hurt the quality of care. The law hurts seniors by cutting $500 billion from Medicare and takes away benefits offered under Medicare Advantage. Tens of thousands of small businesses that cannot afford to buy health insurance will be forced to pay a new IRS-collected tax of $3,000 per employee, which will cause many people to lose their jobs or be forced into part-time work. The law injects government bureaucrats*

between patients and their doctors. This law was a bad idea from the start, and it's still a bad idea.

The Democratic candidate *says the Affordable Care Act is good for America. Health care bills are skyrocketing, companies are dropping plans or forcing employees to pay big deductibles and insurance companies are refusing people with pre-existing conditions. We are finally getting things under control. People with insurance keep their policies and doctors, but will get tax credits to make health care more affordable for the middle class. Insurance companies can't discriminate against you when you get sick. Small businesses will get tax credits if they want to provide health insurance and the uninsured will get access to lower-cost plans and help with premiums. Medicare is protected and seniors pay less for prescription drugs. We finally started to make health care more affordable.*

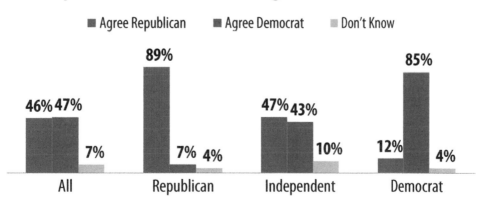

Republican versus Democratic Arguments on ObamaCare

■ Agree Republican   ■ Agree Democrat   ■ Don't Know

Source: Resurgent Republic / Democracy Corps / North Star Opinion Research, National Survey of Likely Voters, July 9-12, 2012

Figure 8-15

That language actually turned a 5-point advantage for opponents of ObamaCare into a 1-point disadvantage. It shows the potency of decades of Democrats bashing health insurance companies in the political debate.

The ObamaCare Rollout Craters Support for the Law

The single-digit opposition to ObamaCare during congressional debate and the first three years after its passage jumped to double digits in most polling during the second half of 2013. With actual implementation, Americans can react to the reality of the law rather than just prospective assertions about its likely effects. And, at least initially, the reality was far more negative than the anticipation.

Three factors drove increasing opposition.

First, the scandals at the Internal Revenue Service targeting conservative groups made implementation of ObamaCare even more problematic given the IRS role in enforcing the individual mandate requiring everyone to have health insurance or pay a fine. Almost six out of ten American voters have little or no trust in the IRS to keep their personal health information private.

Trust in the IRS to Keep Personal Information Private

"How much trust do you have in the IRS managing a database that includes your personal tax and health information and keeping your information private: a great deal, some, not much, or none at all?"

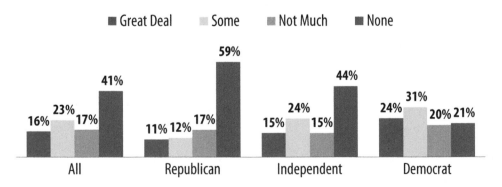

Source: Crossroads GPS / North Star Opinion Research, National Survey of Registered Voters, June 2-5, 2013

Figure 8–16

Second, cancellation of millions of individual health care policies in the fall of 2013 seriously undermined President Obama's credibility based on his repeated assurances that "if you like your health care plan, you can keep it." While those cancellations came as no surprise to those who carefully followed the structure and requirements of the law, they came as a shock to the 64 percent of Americans who believed the president's promise.

Third, the disastrous rollout of the ObamaCare website created enormous frustration, especially among those whose policies had been cancelled. It undermined confidence that the Administration could possibly pull off such a complex and complicated piece of legislation.

The following chart shows the trends in thinking that ObamaCare is a good or bad idea, from the single-digit opposition in 2012 to double-digit opposition in the latter half of 2013. The margin saying the law was a bad rather than a good idea stood at 12 percentage points in May of 2013, 13 points in July, 13 points in September, and 16 points by December.

ObamaCare a Good or Bad Idea: 2012-2014

"Now, as you may know, Barack Obama's health care plan was passed by Congress and signed into law in 2010. From what you have heard about the new health care law, do you think it is a good idea or a bad idea?"

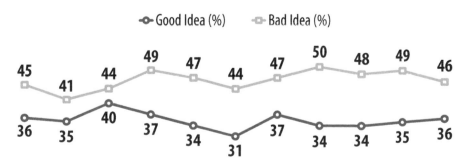

Source: NBC / WSJ

Figure 8–17

The Government Shutdown

Just as health care policies were being cancelled in violation of the president's promise, just as the Healthcare.gov website problems were becoming evident to one and all, Republicans tried to snatch defeat from the jaws of victory. In the face of all evidence to the contrary, against the virtually unanimous warnings of those who had lived through a similar experience before, Republicans shut down the government in a presumed effort to get rid of ObamaCare.

Polling clearly showed beforehand that shutting down the government by attaching repeal to a bill necessary to keep the government running would blow up in the face of Republicans. The picture was obvious as early as June of 2013, and the same views persisted right up to the shutdown on October 1, 2013.

Government Shutdown Good Idea or Bad Idea

"Some people say that the health care reform law is so bad that an effort to repeal it should be attached to a bill necessary to keep the government running. Do you think it is a good idea or a bad idea for opponents of the health care reform law to risk shutting down the government in an effort to get rid of the law?"

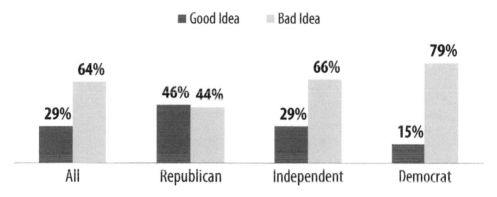

Source: Crossroads GPS / North Star Opinion Research, National Survey of Registered Voters, June 2-5, 2013

Figure 8-18

In contrast to most ObamaCare questions, where Independents think more like Republicans than Democrats, shutting down the government to try to get rid of ObamaCare made Independents look more like Democrats. Moreover, it split Republicans right down the middle. Pursuing a strategy that splits your own base and pushes Independents into the waiting arms of Democrats does not normally lead to victory. And it did not in this case. As seen in the 2012-2014 chart above, shutting down the government actually *increased* the percentage of Americans who thought ObamaCare was a good idea.

Fortunately the incompetence of the ObamaCare rollout came to the Republicans' rescue. After the shutdown ended, public attention refocused on the bumbling Healthcare.gov website, and the growing opposition to ObamaCare was rekindled. But it took a full year for the Republican

Party's favorable rating to recover from the damage caused by the government shutdown in the first two weeks of October 2013.

Republican Party Image and the October 2013 Government Shutdown

"Next, please tell me whether you have a favorable or unfavorable opinion of each of the following parties:"

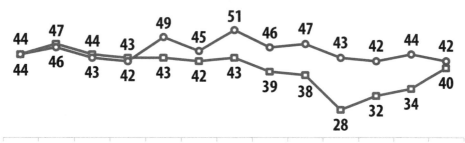

Source: Gallup data from surveys taken 2010-2014. Copyright 2015 Gallup, Inc. All rights reserved.

Figure 8-19

ObamaCare and the 2014 Midterm Elections

In the 2014 midterm elections, ObamaCare faced a raft of criticisms from Republican candidates. Criticisms ran the gamut from the law's effect on costs to its effect on the economy to the way it was passed to its effect on government spending and control.

2014 voters nationally ranked the following as the top criticisms of ObamaCare, with 60 percent or more of likely voters saying each was very persuasive:[60]

To pass ObamaCare, politicians made many promises they knew were not true, like the law will lower your premiums, you can keep your doctor, and Medicare will not be cut.

ObamaCare puts Washington in control of your health care.

ObamaCare takes away choices and forces people to buy coverage they don't want, don't need, and can't afford.

Under ObamaCare, many people are losing their current coverage and being forced into plans with higher deductibles.

ObamaCare drives up health insurance premiums and co-pays.

ObamaCare makes it harder for small businesses to survive by increasing their health care costs.

ObamaCare causes employers to cut back workers' hours from full time to part time to control their health care costs.

ObamaCare will cost American taxpayers more than $2 trillion.

Democratic strategists continually argued in 2014 that running ads on ObamaCare was a waste of money, since all the people who could be persuaded on the issue had already made up their minds. The argument had a certain whistling-past-the-graveyard quality to it, since these same strategists knew how unpopular the law remained.

---

60. Crossroads/GPS & American Action Network/North Star Opinion Research National Survey of Likely 2014 Voters, June 21-29, 2014

Those strategists were wrong. A late September bipartisan survey of the top twelve Senate battleground states showed that the top three issues among likely voters in those states were the economy, ObamaCare, and foreign policy regarding ISIS.[61] One Senate Democrat who voted for the law, Mark Pryor of Arkansas, actually put an ad on TV proclaiming his support and extolling the benefits of ObamaCare. He lost by 17 percentage points, the greatest losing margin of any Democratic senator running for reelection in 2014.

Republican Health Care Messaging in 2015 and Beyond

At this writing the ultimate outcome of ObamaCare is up in the air. The law remains as unpopular as ever. But Democrats are convinced that once some people get health insurance for the first time, and receive government subsidies to buy that insurance, the law will be so rooted in American life that it will be impossible to repeal. Republicans are convinced that ObamaCare is a house of cards, teetering on the brink of collapse, and it is only a matter of time before the entire structure comes crashing down.

While the Administration seems to have finally fixed many of the problems that plagued the Healthcare.gov website, numerous challenges remain:

- Only seventeen states, mostly Democrat-run, have created state-based ObamaCare exchanges for their citizens to obtain insurance.[62] Despite the financial incentives in the law to induce states to set up their own exchanges, most Republican-led states have refused to cooperate, one consequence of the party-line vote used to adopt the law.

---

61. *http://www.npr.org/2014/10/03/353315549/npr-poll-senate-battleground-tilts-republican-but-still-anybodys-game*

62. *http://kff.org/health-reform/state-indicator/state-marketplace-statistics/*

- In the rest of the country, a pending Supreme Court case challenges the subsidies given to people to help them afford insurance,[63] since ObamaCare contains language limiting subsidies to people who sign up in state-based exchanges. So the subsidies promised in the law may never materialize for the vast majority of Americans, thereby dealing a mortal blow to the law.

- The employer mandate that requires employers with more than fifty full-time employees to provide health insurance has been postponed until at least 2015, and substantial pressure will come from the new Republican Congress to eliminate that mandate permanently.

- The individual mandate requiring everyone to buy insurance or face an IRS penalty went into effect in 2014, but time will tell whether the penalty is sufficient to get the previously uninsured to sign up.

- In an effort to limit the political damage coming from the president's promise that "if you like your plan, you can keep it," the Administration allowed people to keep their original plans until 2014, then 2015, then 2016, and now in some cases until 2017, even though those plans do not comply with ObamaCare regulations.[64]

Consequently major provisions of the law have been delayed, postponed, undermined, or challenged in court. ObamaCare is a long way from being fully implemented.

So what should Republicans say in the meantime? What messages on health care will resonate with the American people?

---

63. *http://www.npr.org/blogs/thetwo-way/2014/11/07/362305465/supreme-court-will-hear-case-challenging-obamacare-subsidies*

64. *http://obamacarefacts.com/can-i-keep-my-health-care-plan/*

The answer so far has been full repeal of ObamaCare. If the American people don't like the law, so the argument goes, why not just repeal it? But that answer carries its own pitfalls for two reasons.

First, repealing ObamaCare without a well thought out and coherent alternative allows Democrats to charge:

> *"Republicans want to put the health insurance companies back in charge. They want to allow those companies to discriminate against you if you have a pre-existing condition, cancel your coverage without warning, kick your kids off your policy when they turn 18, and charge you more if you are a woman."*

That charge is powerful because the vast majority of Americans do not want to go back to the system we had before ObamaCare. Only 18 percent say they would like to "go back to the health care system we had before."

Preferred Health Care Option After ObamaCare

"Which of the following comes closer to your view: **A)** We need to keep ObamaCare as is; **B)** We need to keep ObamaCare in place, but continue to make modest changes to the law and fix what is not working; **C)** We need to repeal ObamaCare and go back to the health care system we had before; **D)** We need to repeal ObamaCare and replace it with reforms that lower costs and put patients first?"

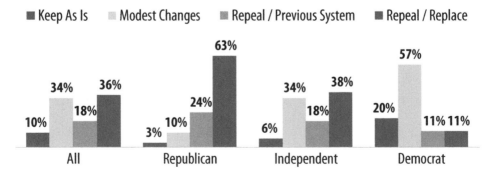

Source: YG Network / North Star Opinion Research, National Survey of Registered Voters, November 4-8, 2014

Figure 8-20

Second, if Republicans truly believe that ObamaCare is bad for their constituents, don't they have an obligation to try to protect their constituents from the worst aspects of the law before they take effect? Voters certainly think so. Consider the following question *asked just of ObamaCare's opponents.*

ObamaCare Opponents Want to Dismantle the Worst Parts Now

"Which of the following comes closest to your view about the best way to stop ObamaCare from harming the health care system: **A)** Opponents of the law should not try to fix the worst parts of ObamaCare now, but wait until they are in a position to repeal the entire law at once. Dismantling it piece-by-piece will only improve ObamaCare and reduce the pressure to get rid of the law entirely; **B)** Opponents of the law should force action to dismantle the worst parts of ObamaCare now, because the earliest they could fully repeal the law would be in 2017 after Obama leaves office, and once the law is implemented it will be even harder to get rid of."

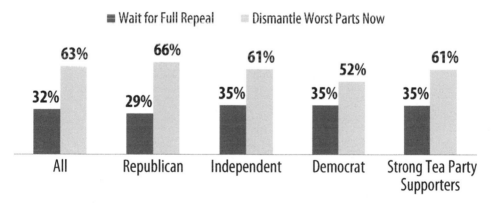

Source: Crossroads GPS / North Star Opinion Research, National Survey of Registered Voters, June 2-5, 2013

Figure 8-21

By a two-to-one margin, opponents of the law want to dismantle the worst parts of the law now rather than wait for full repeal. Note that the question does not use the phrase "fix the worst parts;" Republican voters don't want to "fix" it, they want to "dismantle" it.

The Worst Parts of ObamaCare to Dismantle

ObamaCare is so massive and complex that many provisions work against the American voters' desire for more affordable health care. Following are some of the most promising provisions to be dismantled.

1. Individual mandate

Eliminating the individual mandate would cut a key pillar out from under ObamaCare. While the Supreme Court may have said that the federal government has the authority to require the purchase of health insurance or impose a fine, a majority in all three partisan groups disagrees.

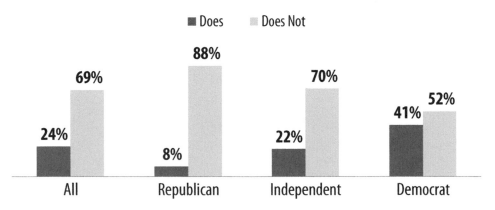

Does the Federal Government have the Authority to Require the Purchase of Health Insurance

"Do you think the federal government does or does not have the authority to require every American to buy health care insurance or pay a fine?"

■ Does   ▨ Does Not

All: 24% / 69%
Republican: 8% / 88%
Independent: 22% / 70%
Democrat: 41% / 52%

Source: YG Policy Center / North Star Opinion Research, National Survey of Registered Voters, March 11-14, 2012

Figure 8–22

2. Medical device taxes

ObamaCare imposed a two percent tax *on the gross revenues* (not the profits) of American companies that make medical devices such as pacemakers, magnetic imaging machines, and ultrasound machines to help fund
the law. Aside from the insanity of taxing gross revenues, which would
still require a company that lost money to pay the tax, the medical device
tax is a clear example of a new tax that will be passed along to consumers,
thus increasing health care costs. Voters across party lines overwhelming
support eliminating the tax.

Voters Want to Eliminate the Medical Device Tax

"Now I would like to ask you about several proposals specifically to change the health
care law passed in 2010. For each of the following, please tell me if you support or
oppose that proposal: Eliminate the new tax on medical devices like pacemakers, MRIs,
and ultrasound machines to lower costs and help American manufacturing."

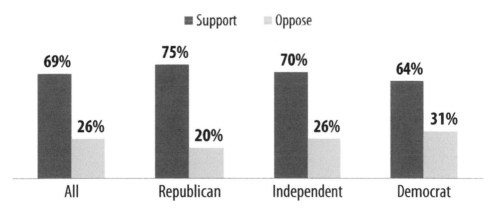

Source: Crossroads GPS / North Star Opinion Research, National Survey of Registered Voters, June 2-5, 2013

Figure 8-23

3. Requirements for comprehensive coverage

ObamaCare requires that any health insurance policies sold on the new health care exchanges cover a wide array of expensive and often undesired benefits that drive the cost of health insurance premiums through the roof. Rather than allow individuals to buy a policy that meets their needs, the new law mandates broad coverage and requires its purchase by people who may prefer more limited catastrophic coverage. Indeed, ObamaCare demands that males, both single and married, purchase maternity coverage! Majorities of Republicans, Independents, and Democrats prefer the freedom and flexibility to purchase policies tailored to them and that they can afford.

Voters Oppose Mandatory Comprehensive Policies

"Which of the following comes closest to your view about the health care law passed in 2010: **A)** We should require that all health insurance policies be comprehensive, covering routine doctor visits and medicines, even though those policies have higher premiums. People do not know what health care needs they will have, and all Americans deserve this level of coverage. **B)** We should allow Americans the flexibility and freedom to buy insurance policies they can afford, even if those policies have more limited coverage. Some people may want just catastrophic coverage for major illnesses and hospital stays, but not for routine doctor visits or medicines."

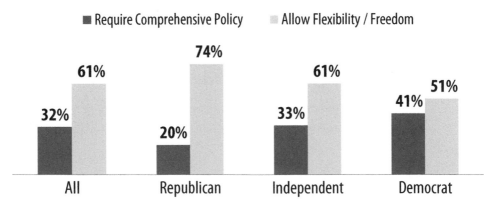

Source: Crossroads GPS / North Star Opinion Research, National Survey of Registered Voters, June 2-5, 2013

Figure 8-24

4. Provisions that jack up health care costs for young and healthy people

Young, healthy people fall directly into the bull's-eye of ObamaCare, with numerous provisions that raise their health insurance premiums. One requirement reduced the amount health insurance companies can charge older, sick people from six times what they charge young, healthy people, down to three times what they can charge young people. The effect will be to drive up health insurance premiums for young people. Young peoples' premiums may go so high that many of them will choose to pay the penalty for not purchasing insurance rather than pay sky-high premiums. Majorities of all three partisan groups support removing that provision.

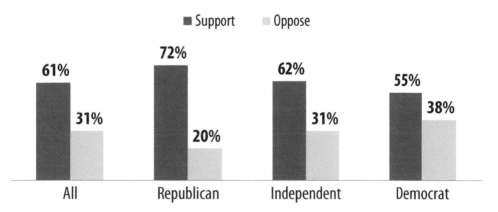

Voters Oppose Requiring the Young to Subsidize the Old

"Now I would like to ask you about several proposals specifically to change the health care law passed in 2010. For each of the following, please tell me if you support or oppose that proposal: Eliminate the upper cap on premiums so that younger people can pay less and are not forced to subsidize health care for older and less healthy Americans."

■ Support ▨ Oppose

	All	Republican	Independent	Democrat
Support	61%	72%	62%	55%
Oppose	31%	20%	31%	38%

Source: Crossroads GPS / North Star Opinion Research, National Survey of Registered Voters, June 2-5, 2013

Figure 8-25

5. Eliminating IPAB, the Independent Payment Advisory Board

The IPAB, famously dubbed "death panels" by Sarah Palin, presents a difficult case. The panel was designed to hold down Medicare costs for seniors, but understanding its role is challenging, and different question wording produces different results. On the one hand, many voters indicate concern about its function.

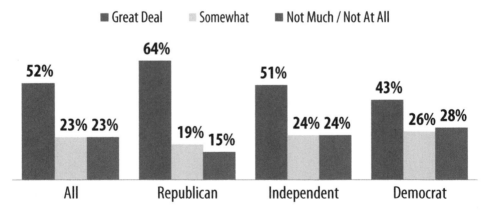

Voters are Concerned that IPAB Will Force Cuts to Medicare

"Now I would like to read you a list of possible outcomes when the health care reform law passed in 2010 is implemented next year. For each of the following, please tell me if that outcome concerns you a great deal, somewhat, not too much, or not at all: The Independent Payment Advisory Board will make automatic cuts to Medicare reimbursement rates that will lead to reduced services for seniors or cause doctors to stop accepting Medicare entirely."

■ Great Deal　　▨ Somewhat　　■ Not Much / Not At All

All: 52%, 23%, 23%
Republican: 64%, 19%, 15%
Independent: 51%, 24%, 24%
Democrat: 43%, 26%, 28%

Source: Crossroads GPS / North Star Opinion Research, National Survey of Registered Voters, June 2-5, 2013

Figure 8–26

But explaining its role produces decidedly mixed results.

But They are Torn About Eliminating IPAB

"Now I would like to ask you about several proposals specifically to change the health care law passed in 2010. For each of the following, please tell me if you support or oppose that proposal: Eliminate the IPAB, an unelected board of 15 bureaucrats who can cut payments for medical procedures if they determine that Medicare is spending too much money."

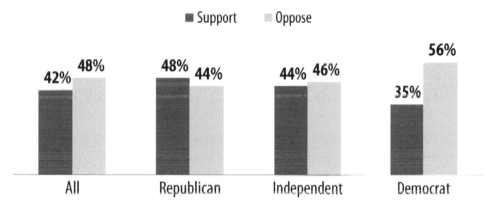

Source: Crossroads GPS / North Star Opinion Research, National Survey of Registered Voters, June 2-5, 2013

Figure 8-27

Here's the bottom line on IPAB: if you have five minutes or more to make your case, then IPAB is a good provision to attack. But if you only have thirty seconds, many other vulnerable points in ObamaCare are easier to explain and understand.

Alternatives to ObamaCare

So what can Republicans offer as alternatives to ObamaCare that are popular among American voters? Following is an array of popular options, all of which are supported by a substantial majority of American voters.

- Keep restrictions on health insurance company practices that voters find so objectionable. Those practices include denying coverage because of pre-existing conditions, cancelling coverage after someone gets sick, setting lifetime limits on coverage, and stopping coverage of children once they reach age 18.

- Allow the sale of less expensive catastrophic policies that are tailored to the needs of individuals, at a price they can afford.

- Expand the use of Health Savings Accounts, HSAs, so that Americans can save pre-tax dollars to help pay the cost of higher deductibles.

- Allow the sale of health insurance policies across state lines to increase competition and drive down prices, similar to the market for automobile insurance. Yes, some health insurance companies say they cannot construct such policies because of variation in insurance regulations state by state. But states have their own automobile insurance regulations as well, and that has not stopped auto insurance companies from selling policies across state lines.

- Allow more involvement of private health insurance companies in Medicare, similar to the Part D prescription drug program. Competition inherent in Part D drove down costs dramatically. Why not try the same with other parts of Medicare?

Dos and Don'ts

Following are some dos and don'ts when discussing health care in the aftermath of ObamaCare:

- **Do** develop a Republican alternative health care reform plan that addresses the most unpopular practices of health insurance companies and focuses on making health care more affordable, the number one priority of the American people.

- **Do** argue for dismantling the worst aspects of ObamaCare now before they have negative effects on your constituents.

- **Do** develop a set of alternative health care policies united by an emphasis on individual freedom and choice, not government mandates.

On the other hand, here are some don'ts:

- **Do not** try to repeal ObamaCare without having a clear and coherent alternative ready to propose and defend.

- **Do not** threaten to shut down the government again in an effort to repeal ObamaCare. That is the one way to turn ObamaCare from a plus to a minus for Republicans.

Conclusion

ObamaCare created a revolution in American health care, a revolution that to this point has never generated majority popular support. But dislike of some of the practices of health insurance companies created fertile ground for ideas like ObamaCare to take root. Consequently there is no going back to "the system we had before."

Constructing a new system that avoids the unpopular practices of the previous system and the pathologies of ObamaCare will be challenging indeed. That will be especially difficult once several million Americans obtain health insurance through the exchanges. But public opinion offers clear support for a set of alternatives that can form the starting point for a new patient-centered system that affords Americans more choice, more options, and more affordable quality health care.

NATIONAL SECURITY *and* AMERICA'S ROLE *in the* WORLD

Rarely does national security or foreign affairs become the central focus of American elections absent a cataclysmic event like 9/11 or unpopular wars like Vietnam and Iraq. But America's role in the world, and the expectation that the president will serve as leader of the free world, always serves as a subtext for American presidential elections. In midterm elections, unexpected world events can force national security and foreign affairs to the top of a political agenda as happened during the summer and fall of 2014 with the rise of the Islamic State.

What does public opinion say about America's role in an uncertain world in the 21st century?

On national security and foreign affairs, far more than on domestic policy, public opinion provides limited guidance in making policy choices. Public opinion sets the range of acceptable policy options, but on foreign affairs that range is exceedingly broad. Elected leaders and foreign policy specialists enjoy great latitude in choosing and building popular support for their preferred policy options.

Public Opinion as a Streambed

Public opinion functions as do the banks of a stream guiding the flow of water. The stream banks determine the acceptable range of policy options—inside the streambed is acceptable, outside is not.

On occasion the streambed narrows precipitously and the range of acceptable policy options for elected officials becomes quite narrow—think attitudes about abortion in a heavily evangelical district in the Deep South, or positions on gay marriage in San Francisco. On those types of issues public opinion is quite stable over time, highly resistant to change, and often quite well-informed on the policy choices in question. Changing the wording of a survey question produces only modest changes in results.

When voters hold stable, strongly-held views on emotional issues of this type, politicians standing on the banks of the stream outside the range of acceptable policy choices face a set of unpalatable options. They can try to change voters' minds, which is extremely difficult on these types of issues. They can change their position on the issue, in the process looking like flip-floppers making a crass political calculation to save their careers. They can try to change the subject, and persuade their constituents that their agreement on other issues outweighs disagreement on this one issue. Or they can prepare to lose gracefully. The last option is not wildly popular among most elected officials.

On many issues, however, the streambed is wide and the range of acceptable policy options quite broad. That characterizes many foreign policy choices such as an appropriate U.S. role in Bosnia, Syria, or Ukraine. While sending U.S. troops to engage directly may have been pushed outside the range of acceptable options at the moment because of long wars in Afghanistan and Iraq, many other options are on the table—bombing, sanctions, arms sales, military advisors, UN resolutions.

On these types of issues public opinion is highly unstable, quite changeable, and often characterized by little knowledge and much misinformation.

Unexpected events can cause large swings in public opinion. Changing the wording of a question can produce dramatically different—and even contradictory—results. Conducting polls on foreign affairs runs the risk of creating, rather than measuring, public opinion.

We got a vivid picture of foreign events rapidly changing public opinion during the summer of 2014. In the year prior to that summer we were informed that "Americans Want to Pull Back from World Stage,"[65] and "Opposition to Air Strikes Surges."[66]

But after the rapid expansion of the Islamic State, or ISIS, and brutal jihadist beheadings of innocent Americans, suddenly the headlines changed: "As New Dangers Loom, More Think the U.S. Does 'Too Little' to Solve World Problems,"[67] "Bipartisan Support for Obama's Military Campaign Against ISIS,"[68] "Almost Two-Thirds Back Attacking Militants."[69]

That is just the most recent example of public opinion shifting rapidly in response to world events. On national security and foreign affairs, great latitude exists for strong leaders to point the way and develop popular support for their preferred policy options.

---

65. *http://online.wsj.com/news/articles/SB10001424052702304163604579532050055966782#*

66. *http://www.people-press.org/2013/09/09/opposition-to-syrian-airstrikes-surges/*

67. *http://www.people-press.org/2014/08/28/as-new-dangers-loom-more-think-the-u-s-does-too-little-to-solve-world-problems/*

68. *http://www.people-press.org/2014/09/15/bipartisan-support-for-obamas-military-campaign-against-isis/*

69. *http://online.wsj.com/articles/wsj-nbc-poll-finds-that-almost-two-thirds-of-americans-back-attacking-militants-1410301920?mod=WSJ_hp_LEFTTopStories*

American Involvement in the World

American public opinion has long held an isolationist streak, with the extent of isolationist sentiment driven by world events and national leadership. Popular resistance kept America out of World War II until Pearl Harbor left the country no choice. September 11 forced American involvement in Afghanistan where otherwise we would never have been so deeply engaged. But absent cataclysmic events, an appeal to focus on our problems here at home has consistent popular appeal.

Public Wants to Keep Focus at Home

"We should not think so much in international terms but concentrate more on our own national problems and building up our own strengths and prosperity here at home."

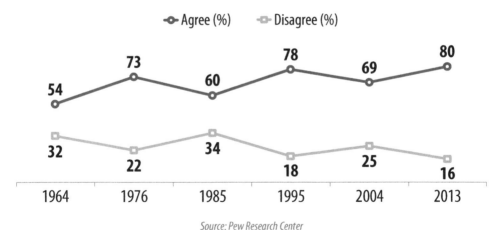

Source: Pew Research Center

Figure 9–1

But note the wording of that question: "concentrate more on our own national problems." When international affairs create "national problems" for America, as with Pearl Harbor and 9/11, public opinion can shift rapidly. That is why any elected official making the case for American involvement in the world needs to link that involvement to solving or avoiding "national problems" here at home.

That may be one reason why a more explicit call for the U.S. to "mind its own business" produces a very different picture.

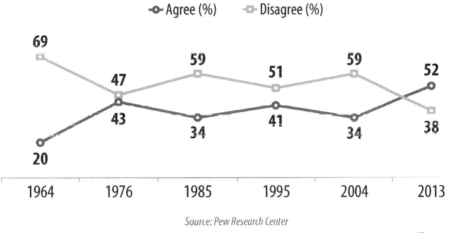

Majority Says U.S. Should 'Mind Its Own Business Internationally'

"The U.S. should mind its own business internationally and let other countries get along the best they can on their own."

-○- Agree (%)   -□- Disagree (%)

69
59   59
47   51   52
43   41   38
34   34
20

1964   1976   1985   1995   2004   2013

Source: Pew Research Center

Figure 9-2

This polling result created quite a stir in 2013 when, for the first time since 1964, a majority of Americans agreed that we should "mind our own business." But answers to other questions with different wording point in a different direction, and show the limits of isolationist sentiment among Americans.

International events have a nasty habit of intruding into "our own business" in ways that it is impossible for the only remaining superpower to avoid. Perhaps that is why Americans in 2013 showed no appetite for completely pulling in our horns. Americans of all partisan persuasions still want the U.S. to remain the only military superpower.

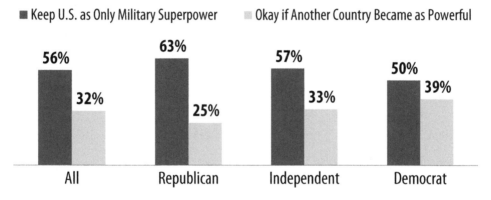

Public Wants U.S. to Remain Sole Military Superpower

"In the future, should U.S. policies try to keep it so America is the only military superpower, OR would it be acceptable if China, another country or the European Union became as militarily powerful as the U.S.?"

■ Keep U.S. as Only Military Superpower   ▨ Okay if Another Country Became as Powerful

Source: Pew Research Center, November 2013

Figure 9–3

Americans' Priorities in Foreign Affairs

Americans' priorities in foreign affairs reflect that desire to protect our own. The top priorities in foreign affairs have been stable and consistent since the 1990s, with protecting our lives and our jobs at the top of the list, and improving life in other countries at the bottom.

Public's Long-Range Foreign Policy Goals

"How much priority do you think the U.S. should give to each of the following long-range foreign policy goals?"

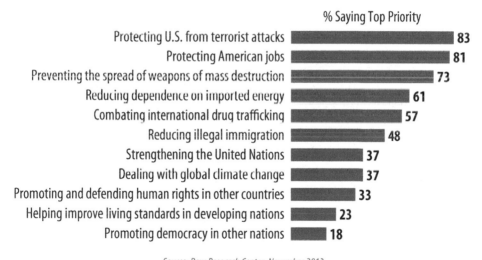

% Saying Top Priority

Protecting U.S. from terrorist attacks	83
Protecting American jobs	81
Preventing the spread of weapons of mass destruction	73
Reducing dependence on imported energy	61
Combating international drug trafficking	57
Reducing illegal immigration	48
Strengthening the United Nations	37
Dealing with global climate change	37
Promoting and defending human rights in other countries	33
Helping improve living standards in developing nations	23
Promoting democracy in other nations	18

Source: Pew Research Center, November 2013

Figure 9–4

When asked to name the top foreign threats to America, various threats to our lives once again top the list.

Extremist Groups, Other Countries' Nuclear Programs Seen as Major Threats

"I'd like your opinion about some possible international concerns for the U.S. Do you think that _____ is a major threat, a minor threat or not a threat to the well-being of the United States?"

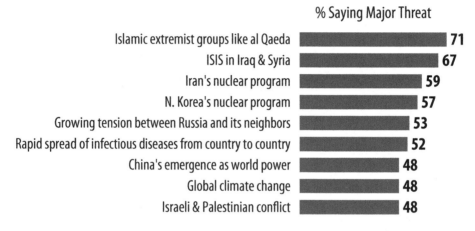

% Saying Major Threat

Islamic extremist groups like al Qaeda	71
ISIS in Iraq & Syria	67
Iran's nuclear program	59
N. Korea's nuclear program	57
Growing tension between Russia and its neighbors	53
Rapid spread of infectious diseases from country to country	52
China's emergence as world power	48
Global climate change	48
Israeli & Palestinian conflict	48

Source: Pew Research Center, August 2014

Figure 9-5

American Support for Aggressive Efforts to Protect the Country

Given that Americans feel our top priority should be protecting the nation from terrorist attacks, and that extremist Islamists are seen as our greatest threat, Americans give their leaders wide latitude in keeping the country safe. That is why techniques that cause widespread angst in other countries enjoy strong popular support here at home.

Despite ongoing debate and controversy about the methods, Americans overwhelmingly believe the CIA's use of harsh interrogation techniques in its efforts to gain information from captured terrorists is justified. A majority of Americans has consistently believed that the CIA's methods were justified in the wake of 9/11.

Americans Believe Treatment of Suspected Terrorists Was Justified

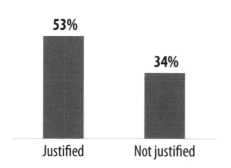

"Based on what you have read or heard, would you say harsh interrogation of detainees was justified or not justified?"

"All in all, do you think the CIA's treatment of suspected terrorists was justified or unjustified?"

Source: Resurgent Republic / North Star Opinion Research, May 2009

Source: ABC News / Washington Post Poll, December 2014

Figure 9-6

Support for harsh interrogation is sustained even when faced with powerful arguments criticizing those techniques.

Americans Believe Harsh Interrogation May Sometimes Be Necessary

"**Congressman A** says America should never use harsh interrogation techniques on detainees, because they are torture. Those techniques undermine our values, hurt our standing in the world, endanger American troops who might be taken prisoner, and yield little or no useful information that could not be obtained by other means.

Congressman B says that, while harsh interrogation techniques of detainees should be used only rarely, they may be necessary in exceptional situations to protect the country. Those techniques are justified when they are the only way to stop the murder of another 3000 innocent Americans in another 9/11."

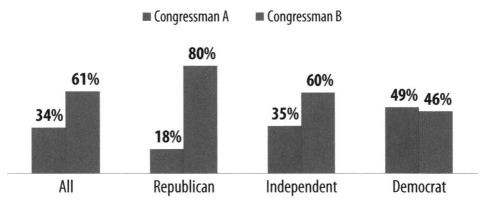

Source: Resurgent Republic / North Star Opinion Research, May 2009

Figure 9-7

Part of the reason Americans believe those techniques are justified is that they believe harsh interrogation has yielded crucial information that could not have been obtained otherwise.

Americans Think Harsh Interrogation is Effective at Saving Lives

"Congressman A says harsh interrogation of detainees is not effective. It yields little useful information that could not have been obtained by traditional interrogation methods. Harsh interrogation makes detainees lie to stop the harsh treatment. While traditional methods might take more time, they are more effective in the long run.

Congressman B says harsh interrogation of detainees is effective. Khalid Sheikh Mohammed, the mastermind of 9/11, refused to talk to interrogators under traditional interrogation methods, and disclosed information about planned attacks only after being waterboarded many times. American lives were saved by using these enhanced techniques."

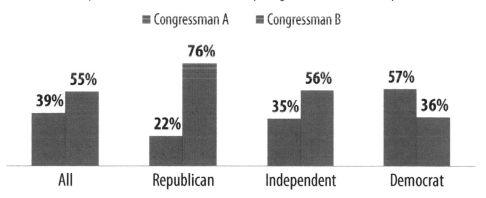

Source: Resurgent Republic / North Star Opinion Research, May 2009

Figure 9-8

In addition to finding harsh techniques justified and effective, Americans support the use of drones to kill terrorists in other countries, with half of voters believing drones have made the country safer and only a small minority believing they have made the country less safe.

Americans Believe Drones Have Made the Country Safer

"Has [the] use of military drones made U.S. safer from terrorism, less safe or hasn't it made a difference?"

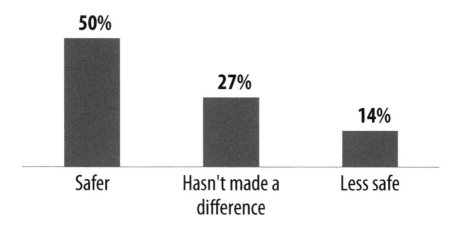

Source: Pew Research Center, November 2013

Figure 9-9

When it comes to national security and protecting the country from terrorist attacks, public opinion gives public officials extraordinarily wide latitude in devising the means to keep the country safe. Numerous options will be supported so long as public officials can make a compelling case that a particular technique will advance the cause of safety and security.

Perceptions of America's Current Standing in the World

After six years of Barack Obama, Americans view their country as playing a far less important and powerful role in the world than it did ten years earlier.

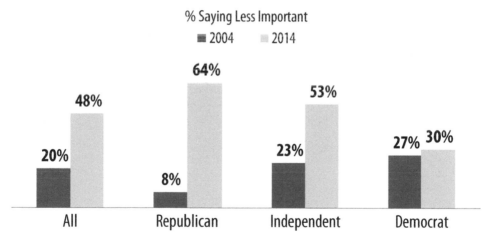

Americans Think the U.S. is Less Important as a World Leader Today

"Do you think the United States plays a more important and powerful role as a world leader today compared to 10 years ago, a less important role, or about as important a role as a world leader as it did 10 years ago?"

% Saying Less Important
■ 2004   ■ 2014

	All	Republican	Independent	Democrat
2004	20%	8%	23%	27%
2014	48%	64%	53%	30%

Source: Pew Research Center / USA Today

Figure 9–10

Despite the fact that Americans perceive the U.S. as having a diminished role in the world, they still believe that America remains the world's dominant military power."

Public Views U.S. as Leading Military Power...

"Which is the leading *military* power?"

	Nov 2009	Jan 2011	Nov 2013
United States	63%	67%	68%
China	18%	16%	14%
Russia	6%	5%	6%
EU countries	2%	3%	2%
Other (Vol.)/DK	11%	9%	8%

Source: Pew Research Center

Figure 9-11

On the other hand, they perceive that economic leadership has passed to other countries, especially China.

...and China as Top Economic Power

"Which is the world's leading *economic* power?"

	Feb 2008	Nov 2009	Jan 2011	Nov 2013
China	30%	44%	47%	48%
United States	41%	27%	31%	31%
Japan	10%	13%	9%	8%
EU countries	9%	5%	6%	5%
Other (Vol.)/DK	10%	11%	7%	7%

Source: Pew Research Center

Figure 9–12

Perceptions of the Role America Should Play in the World

Even after a decade of war in Afghanistan and Iraq, Americans clearly do not want their country to be a follower in world affairs, or to present an image of weakness. Indeed, over the course of the Obama presidency, the desire for a president who will present an image of strength to the world has *increased*:

Desire for a President to Present an Image of Strength has Grown During the Obama Years

"Thinking now about America's image abroad, please tell me which of the following statements you agree with more? **A)** We need a president who will present an image that America has a more open approach and is willing to negotiate with friends and foes alike; **B)** We need a president who will present an image of strength that shows America's willingness to confront our enemies and stand up for our principles."

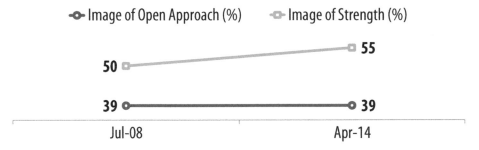

(Note: In 2008, question language read "When it comes to re-establishing America's image abroad, there are two viewpoints concering what would be better to re-establish America's image in other countries. Please tell me which one you agree with more.")

Source: Hart Research Associates / Public Opinion Strategies

Figure 9–13

Similarly, the proportion of people who think Obama has been "not tough enough" on foreign policy and national security has increased, and the proportion who think he has been "about right" has declined.

More Say Obama is 'Not Tough Enough' than 'About Right' on National Security

"Do you think Barack Obama is too tough, not tough enough, or about right in his approach to foreign policy and national security issues?"

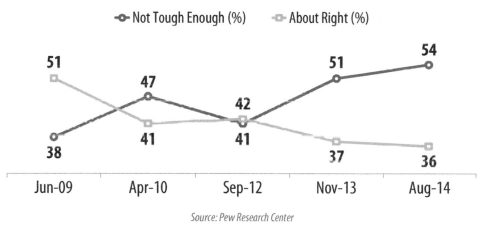

Source: Pew Research Center

Figure 9–14

Any lingering reluctance to get involved militarily overseas does not extend to economic involvement, where support has actually increased in recent years. Americans apparently perceive the global economy as here to stay and our active role in that economy as necessary to grow American jobs.

Two-Thirds Say Greater U.S. Involvement in Global Economy Is a Good Thing

"Greater U.S. involvement in global economy is a..."

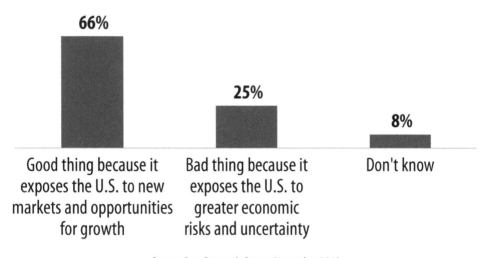

66%	25%	8%
Good thing because it exposes the U.S. to new markets and opportunities for growth	Bad thing because it exposes the U.S. to greater economic risks and uncertainty	Don't know

Source: Pew Research Center, November 2013

Figure 9-15

War fatigue of the past decade does not translate into an across-the-board desire to withdraw from the world. Americans believe that our involvement in the economic sphere is not just inevitable, but desirable.

The NSA Surveillance Program

In contrast to consistent public opinion on the broad goals of national security, foreign affairs, and America's role in the world, questions on the National Security Agency surveillance program to collect telephone and internet data to fight terrorism fall at the other end of the spectrum. On this issue public opinion is unstable and characterized by little knowledge and much misinformation.

The NSA program pits two important values against each other: privacy and security. On the one hand, Americans are suspicious of the federal government getting too powerful and invading their privacy. On the other hand, they want the federal government to protect them from terrorist threats. So questions on this program essentially ask people how they balance the two competing and desirable goals. The result is that questions with somewhat different wording can produce remarkably different outcomes.

On June 6-9, 2013, Pew Research conducted a survey on the NSA program shortly after its existence was revealed by Edward Snowden. That survey showed that, by a margin of 56 to 41 percent, Americans believed that it is *acceptable* for the NSA to get "secret court orders to track calls of millions of Americans to investigate terrorism."[70]

But a Gallup survey conducted only four days later showed that, by a margin of 53 to 37 percent, Americans *disapproved* of the program: "As part of its efforts to investigate terrorism, a federal government agency obtained records from larger U.S. telephone and internet companies in order to compile telephone call logs and internet communications."[71]

The Pew Research Center was so struck by how much views on this program changed depending on question wording that it conducted an experiment testing the effects of different wording.[72] The key phrases affecting support for the program are:

---

70. *http://www.people-press.org/2013/06/10/majority-views-nsa-phone-tracking-as-acceptable-anti-terror-tactic/*

71. *http://www.gallup.com/poll/163043/americans-disapprove-government-surveillance-programs.aspx*

72. *http://www.people-press.org/2013/07/26/government-surveillance-a-question-wording-experiment/*

- Whether court approval is or is not mentioned.

- Whether the program is linked to anti-terrorism efforts.

- Whether the type of data collected is metadata such as date, time, and phone numbers or email addresses, or actual recordings of telephone calls and texts of emails.

Combining the most favorable words into one question increased support for the NSA program by a full 25 percentage points.[73]

Opinions on the NSA program are also characterized by substantial misinformation. When asked what data the government is collecting under the program, 63 percent thought the government is collecting "what is being said in phone calls and emails," including 27 percent who thought the government "has listened to *your* calls or read *your* emails."[74] No credible evidence has ever been produced to support the assertion that the NSA program has collected the content of calls and emails of ordinary American citizens.

In addition, opinions on NSA surveillance are affected by partisanship. Republicans and Democrats react differently to government efforts depending on the party controlling the White House at the time. When George W. Bush was president, Republicans overwhelmingly approved of the NSA secretly listening to phone calls and reading emails of people suspected of being involved in terrorism and Democrats were overwhelmingly opposed. But when Barack Obama was president, Republicans were split and Democrats overwhelmingly supported the NSA "getting secret court orders to track calls of millions of Americans to investigate terrorism."

---

73. Ibid.

74. *http://www.people-press.org/2013/07/26/few-see-adequate-limits-on-nsa-surveillance-program/*

Republican and Democratic Views of NSA Surveillance Depend on Who is President: Bush in 2006 versus Obama in 2013

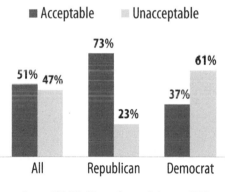

"... as you may know, the NSA has been investigating people suspected of involvement with terrorism by secretly listening in on telephone calls and reading emails between some people in the US and other countries, without first getting court approval to do so. Would you consider this wiretapping of telephone calls and emails without court approval as an acceptable or unacceptable way for the federal government to investigate terrorism?"

■ Acceptable ▨ Unacceptable

All: 51% 47%
Republican: 73% 23%
Democrat: 37% 61%

Source: ABC / Washington Post, early January 2006

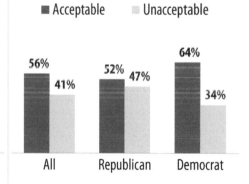

"As you may know, it has been reported that the NSA has been getting secret court orders to track telephone call records of millions of Americans in an effort to investigate terrorism. Would you consider this access to telephone call records an acceptable or unacceptable way for the federal government to investigate terrorism?"

■ Acceptable ▨ Unacceptable

All: 56% 41%
Republican: 52% 47%
Democrat: 64% 34%

Source: Pew Research Center, June 2013

Figure 9–16

Surveys about the NSA surveillance program show the limits of using public opinion to determine important questions of foreign policy. While opinion research does provide important guidance on broad goals and priorities, it is of little use when making decisions about specific foreign policy or national security decisions. That is the province of elected leaders and military experts who have substantial latitude to build popular support for their preferred policy options.

Dos and Don'ts

Following are some dos and don'ts for candidates and elected officials when discussing national security, foreign affairs, and America's role in the world.

- **Do** argue for a responsible leadership role for America in world affairs—not reckless, not unilateral, not headstrong, but responsible. Most Americans understand that problems overseas do not go away just because we ignore them. They understand that the only country capable of assembling the broad coalitions necessary to combat terrorism and other evils is the United States. And they understand that waiting for other countries to take the lead is a formula for endless delay.

- **Do** argue that privacy is important, but security is more so. Americans value their privacy and officials should be sensitive to that concern, but they should place protection from terrorists higher on the priority list, because that is the most important foreign policy goal for most Americans.

- **Do** argue for foreign affairs priorities in terms directly linked to domestic concerns. That should not be a difficult task given the interconnected nature of the global economy and America's role as the only remaining superpower. Almost any foreign affairs initiative can be tied to our security, our safety and our jobs. Answer the question, "Why is it in America's self-interest to do this?"

- **Do** anticipate that events can drive rapid changes in public opinion on national security and foreign affairs. Far more than on issues like abortion, where opinions have been stable for decades, international events can cause rapid shifts in public opinion, especially those that appear to be threats to the United States. Therein lies the danger in an isolationist stance, because events can make a politician espousing that position seem quickly out of touch and behind the times.

On the other hand, here are some don'ts:

- **Do not** argue for American withdrawal from world affairs. Most Americans, and certainly most members of the center-right coalition, are not isolationists. Indeed, they want America to play a leading role in the world, not recklessly, and certainly not without partners and allies, but they do want this country to lead. "Leading from behind,"[75] an Obama advisor's unfortunate phrase, sounds a lot like "following." Most Americans do not want this country to "follow" anyone.

- **Do not** make the case for American involvement in the world from a moral imperative to help less fortunate countries. That is a noble goal for the many humanitarian missions where Americans have done enormous good around the world for decades. But given the myriad problems facing America here at home, making the case for American foreign affairs initiatives in moral or humanitarian terms gains little traction in public opinion.

Even more than in domestic policies, Americans look to their elected officials for leadership in national security and foreign affairs. Most Americans' limited knowledge about the rest of the world gives our leaders greater latitude to define a vision for America's role in the world, and persuade voters to support them to implement that vision.

---

75. *http://www.washingtonpost.com/opinions/the-obama-doctrine-leading-from-behind/2011/04/28/AFBCy18E_story.html*

★ CONCLUSION ★

A REPUBLICAN MESSAGE *for the* NEW AMERICA

The 2010 and 2014 midterm elections offered Republicans hope after the devastating presidential election losses of 2008 and 2012. Senate victories in swing states like Colorado and Iowa; gubernatorial victories in blue states like Illinois, Maryland, and Massachusetts; and state legislative victories throughout the country demonstrate that Republicans can be competitive throughout the nation, not just in deeply red states. The combination of strong candidates, smart strategies, an unpopular president in the sixth year of his term, an unpopular overhaul of the health care system, more favorable electoral demographics in midterm elections, and a disproportionate number of U.S. Senate seats up in red and purple states presented Republicans with a golden opportunity of which they took fullest advantage.

Unfortunately none of those factors alter the long-term forces that create such challenges for Republican candidates at the presidential level. The worst mistake would be to read the victories of 2010 and 2014 as an indication that Republicans can elect presidents in the new America without making significant changes.

As mentioned in the Introduction, there is no one "correct" answer to the changes that will lead to greater Republican presidential success. But there clearly are directions that are promising, and others that lead to dead ends.

Republicans have no need to throw out their fundamental principles. America remains a center-right country, and the party that stands for individual liberty, free enterprise, limited government, personal responsibility, and expanded opportunity for all has an advantage in this country. But the fundamental principles need to be adapted and communicated to a rapidly changing America.

Following are a few steps that will help the Republican Party adapt its message to the America of the 21st century.

1. Recognize the problem.

The first step is recognizing the need for change. Acknowledge that the Republican message that worked so well in presidential elections in the second half of the 20th century will not work in this century. That is the critical first step.

Recognizing a problem is often emotionally and psychologically challenging. Denial is a natural tendency. Many Republicans are attached to the old messages, the old phrases, and—frankly—the old America. Many do not like the changes they see all around them and strongly resist. Mississippi U.S. Senate candidate Chris McDaniel put it well in 2014 when he said: "Millions in this country feel like strangers in this land. You recognize that, don't you? An older America is passing away. A newer America is rising to take its place. We recoil from that culture. It's foreign to us. It's offensive to us."[76]

The challenge for Republicans is that McDaniel was exactly right: "An older America is passing away. A newer America is rising to take its place." And future presidents will be elected by that newer America.

Just as the business that invested heavily in the sale and rental of video tapes needed to recognize and deal with the threat of Netflix and streaming video, so must Republicans recognize and deal with the threat of demographic change. If the business model is worn out, adopt a new business model for a new world. Or go the way of the video tape.

---

76. *http://online.wsj.com/news/articles/SB100014240527023046401045794879807939 71554?mg=reno64-wsj*

2. Believe that the Republican message of opportunity for all works regardless of the voters' race, color, creed, or national origin.

Republicans should take their message of individual liberty, free enterprise, limited government, and expanded opportunity for all to anyone who might listen, not just those they are sure will listen. Many Republicans give lip service to their principles applying to all kinds of people, but their actions belie their words. When Republicans do not campaign in non-white communities, when they do not advertise on Spanish-language media, when—even worse—they campaign against ethnic minorities, their actions suggest that Republican values and principles cannot be successful in non-white communities. Ronald Reagan did not believe that, and neither should we.

3. Drive down the middle of the right-hand side of the road.

Successful Republican candidates drive down the middle of the right-hand side of the road. If they veer too far to the right, they run into the ditch. If they veer too far to the left, they run into a Democrat posing as a moderate coming the other way. The safest and most successful route to Republican electoral success lies in the middle of the right-hand side of the road.

American voters as a whole reject extremes. While they want their politicians to have a clear sense of direction, a rudder for their journey, they reject what appears to be ideological rigidity. Successful Republicans make Democrats defend the extreme positions promoted by the far-left wing of their party rather than defending positions promoted by the far-right wing of their own.

4. Offer more grace, less condemnation.

Too many Republicans come across as judgmental prophets, condemning sinners to roast in hell for all eternity. Any message will be far more readily accepted if offered in a spirit of grace and acceptance. In Christian terms, Republicans need more New Testament, less Old Testament, more Jesus, less Pharisee.

Whether the topic is abortion, gay rights, or immigration, tone is absolutely critical. People will not vote for a candidate they think perceives them as hopeless sinners who should be written off. Even when they disagree with a candidate's position on an issue, voters may still support that candidate if they think he or she views their challenges with sympathy and concern.

Put another way, voters don't care what you know unless they know that you care.

5. Be for limited government, not no government.

Most Americans see a legitimate role for government, from establishing a national defense to building transportation infrastructure to running public schools to providing Social Security to restraining the worst impulses of the private sector. Questioning the legitimacy of government providing any of those benefits is a sure way to define a candidate as outside the mainstream of American political thought.

That is certainly not to say that government is the answer to all our problems. Americans do not believe it is. The Obama campaign's *Life of Julia* discussed in Chapter 3 crossed the line. The answer is *limited* government that leaves plenty of room for individual initiative, entrepreneurial endeavor, and personal responsibility.

6. Create a positive agenda focused on the future.

Real leaders propose thoughtful and forward-looking ideas to confront the problems facing our nation. The best political candidates develop a creative set of ideas to be *for*, as well as a list of bad ideas to be *against*. It is easy to make a list of all those things Republicans are against—it is far more difficult to make a list of those things they are for. Strong candidates craft a positive set of ideas, and argue the virtue of those ideas with a level of detail that goes well beyond talking points.

We all want to believe that candidates run for office to do something good for the country. Candidates who give voters a clear sense of where they want to take the country are more likely to win elections.

7. Remember that hope and optimism beat despair and pessimism.

Part of Ronald Reagan's political genius was infusing conservative principles with an uplifting sense of hope and optimism. We want our presidents to inspire us with a belief that our challenges are manageable, no matter how great they might be. We want our presidents to paint a vision of a better America whose best days still lie ahead.

Republican presidential candidates need to offer a compelling, hopeful, and optimistic vision for a better life.

Checklist for a Successful Republican Presidential Candidate in 2016

Following is a checklist for a Republican presidential candidate who can win the 2016 general election. A candidate who can honestly answer "yes" to most of these questions stands a very good chance of being competitive against the Democratic nominee. A candidate who answers "no" to most of them needs to do something other than run for president in 2016.

1. Is the candidate positive, hopeful, and optimistic?

Whether the candidate is Ronald Reagan, George H. W. Bush, or George W. Bush, successful Republican candidates offer a positive, hopeful, and optimistic outlook for America and a vision of a better life for everyone.

2. Does the candidate hold, or has he or she recently held, major political office?

Since the founding of the nation our presidents have all met one of three criteria:

- A Founding Father

- A victorious military commander

- A current or former major political office holder

No one today can meet the first criterion. There is no Dwight D. Eisenhower or Ulysses S. Grant on the horizon who can meet the second. That means a credible candidate for president will have experience in major political office. If the candidate is a current or former vice president, cabinet member, governor, senator, or leader in the House of Representatives, then that candidate is potentially credible as a candidate for president. If not, the candidate is wasting his or her time and everyone else's.

3. Does the candidate offer a specific and persuasive agenda to appeal to the economic anxieties of the middle class?

The economic recovery following the 2008 recession has been so anemic, and has offered so few tangible benefits to the middle class, that economic anxiety remains rampant some six years into the recovery. Any successful presidential candidate must craft a specific plan that can offer real promise of economic recovery for the besieged middle class.

4. Does the candidate appeal to Hispanics and other minority voters?

A Republican with any hope of winning the presidency in 2016 must achieve about 30 percent of the non-white vote overall (up from Romney's 17 percent in 2012), including close to a majority of the Hispanic vote (up from Romney's 27 percent). That means using an inclusive tone and reaching out aggressively to minority communities. It also means crafting a position on immigration reform that sends a signal that Republicans really want Hispanics as part of the center-right coalition.

5. Does the candidate appeal to blue-collar white voters?

A successful Republican in 2016 must be attractive to blue-collar white voters, and must have empathy for the challenges that blue-collar families face in an economy with a declining number of manufacturing jobs.

6. Does the candidate appeal to young people?

Appealing to young people has nothing to do with the age of the candidate. Ronald Reagan, our oldest president to date, was exceedingly popular among young people, so much so that Democrats in 1988 bemoaned the prospect of ever winning them back.

An optimistic outlook and a vision for a growing economy will help attract young people. A candidate attractive to the younger generations must also avoid coming across like a cultural Neanderthal, and that means not being hostile to gay Americans. While he or she does not necessarily need to endorse gay marriage, a candidate who comes across as anti-gay will never connect with under-30 voters in this new America.

7. Can the candidate win critical swing states, especially those where Republicans hold major statewide office?

Just as they did in the Senate races of 2014, Republicans must expand the map and increase the number of states that could fall into the Republican column if they are to have any hope of winning the presidency in 2016. A good place to start are states that voted for Obama in 2008 or 2012 but where Republicans hold major statewide office—governor or U.S. senator.

States that voted for Obama at least once where Republicans hold two of the three major statewide offices include Florida, Iowa, Illinois, Indiana, Maine, North Carolina, Nevada, Ohio, and Wisconsin. Those states contain a treasure trove of 119 electoral votes, and would have been more than enough to swing both the 2008 and 2012 presidential elections to the Republicans.

A more ambitious list includes eight Obama states where Republicans hold one major statewide office. That list comprises Colorado, Maryland, Massachusetts, Michigan, New Hampshire, New Jersey, New Mexico, and Pennsylvania. Leaving aside Maryland and Massachusetts, where Republicans have not been competitive in presidential elections for many years, the remaining six states hold another 68 electoral votes. That yields a total of 187 electoral votes where a strong Republican presidential candidate could potentially be competitive.

8. Can the candidate unite the various factions of the Republican coalition: business people, social conservatives, tea partiers, libertarians, and internationalists?

No one faction is sufficiently large to dominate the Republican coalition, so a successful candidate will be—if not wildly popular—at least acceptable to each of the five major groups that make up the modern Republican

Party. Uniting the Republican coalition is the first step to winning the general election.

Ronald Reagan's Vision

Ronald Reagan truly believed that the Republican ideals of individual liberty, free markets, and limited government know no ethnic boundaries. He viewed America as a land of opportunity for all, regardless of race, color, or creed. And he believed that the Republican message would be persuasive to all who wanted to work hard to better their lives.

He spelled out his vision of A Shining City on a Hill in his farewell address to the nation in 1989.

I've spoken of the shining city all my political life, but I don't know if I ever quite communicated what I saw when I said it. But in my mind it was a tall, proud city built on rocks stronger than oceans, windswept, God-blessed, and teeming with people of all kinds living in harmony and peace; a city with free ports that hummed with commerce and creativity. And if there had to be city walls, the walls had doors and the doors were open to anyone with the will and the heart to get here. That's how I saw it, and see it still.

And how stands the city on this winter night? More prosperous, more secure, and happier than it was eight years ago. But more than that: After 200 years, two centuries, she still stands strong and true on the granite ridge, and her glow has held steady no matter what storm. And she's still a beacon, still a magnet for all who must have freedom, for all the pilgrims from all the lost places who are hurtling through the darkness, toward home.[77]

A city "teeming with people of all kinds living in harmony and peace." "And if there had to be city walls, the walls had doors and the doors were

---

77. *http://www.presidency.ucsb.edu/ws/?pid=29650*

open to anyone with the will and the heart to get here." America is "still a beacon, still a magnet for all who must have freedom, for all the pilgrims from all the lost places who are hurtling through the darkness, toward home."

That hardly characterizes the tone of many Republicans talking about the new America today. But that is the optimism, the inclusiveness, and the hopefulness that built the last large Republican majority in this country. And it can do so again.

ABOUT THE AUTHOR

Whit Ayres is a leading Washington, D.C. political consultant with over 30 years of experience in polling and survey research for high profile political campaigns, corporations, and non-profit organizations.

Ayres is the founder and president of North Star Opinion Research (*www.northstaropinion.com*), a national public opinion and public affairs research firm located in Alexandria, Virginia. North Star provides strategic recommendations and advice on messaging to high level political clients including Tennessee Governor Bill Haslam and U.S. Senators Marco Rubio, Lamar Alexander, Bob Corker, Lindsey Graham, and Jim Inhofe. Ayres has also worked with numerous non-profit clients including the Boy Scouts of America, the U.S. Chamber of Commerce, America's Health Insurance Plans, and the Pharmaceutical Care Management Association.

Ayres and former RNC Chairman Ed Gillespie are cofounders of Resurgent Republic (*www.resurgentrepublic.com*), a center-right non-profit which develops national polls and focus groups and disseminates the results, helping policy makers, think tanks, interest groups, and others advocate for policies that are consistent with conservative principles. Resurgent's research is regularly cited by leading journalists and politicos.

Ayres has been active in The American Association of Political Consultants (*www.theaapc.org*) for over 20 years, serving as its chairman, president, and treasurer. In 2012 Ayres was honored as the Republican Pollster of the Year by the organization. AAPC is a bi-partisan professional society that promotes the political consulting industry, protects political freedom of speech, and fosters ethical behavior in political campaigns.

Ayres is a frequent commentator on network and cable media outlets, including NBC's *Meet the Press*, FOX News, CNN, and NPR. His comments and analysis appear in *The Wall Street Journal*, *The New York Times*, *The Washington Post*, *The Los Angeles Times*, *USA Today*, and numerous regional newspapers.

Ayres founded North Star after a career as a tenured professor in the Department of Government and International Studies at the University of South Carolina. He is a graduate of Davidson College and holds a Ph.D. in political science from the University of North Carolina at Chapel Hill.

All profits from the sale of *2016 and Beyond* will be contributed to Resurgent Republic.

ABOUT RESURGENT REPUBLIC

Resurgent Republic is a 501(c)(4) organization dedicated to shaping the debate over the proper role of government. Resurgent Republic is an independent, not-for-profit organization that conducts public opinion research, and makes the results public through its website (*www.resurgentrepublic.com*), press releases, press conferences, and various publications.

Resurgent Republic helps policy makers, think tanks, interest groups, and others advocate for policies that are consistent with conservative principles, and oppose policies that stifle job creation, weaken national security, and undermine values that have made America a great country.

Former RNC Chairman Ed Gillespie and GOP pollster Whit Ayres founded Resurgent Republic in 2009.

CPSIA information can be obtained at www.ICGtesting.com
Printed in the USA
LVOW02s2258071015

457405LV00019B/32/P